No Other Country

No Other Country

Al Purdy

McCLELLAND AND STEWART

Copyright©1977 by Al Purdy
All rights reserved
ISBN: 0-7710-7208-2

The Canadian Publishers
McClelland and Stewart Limited
25 Hollinger Road, Toronto

Canadian Cataloguing in Publication Data

Purdy, Alfred W., 1918-
  No other country

ISBN 0-7710-7208-2

I. Title.

PS8531.U73N58   C814'.5'4   C77-001352-X
PR9199.3.P87N58

Printed and bound in Canada
by John Deyell Company

For Jacko Onalik
and Martin Senigak

Books by Al Purdy

The Enchanted Echo (1944)
Pressed on Sand (1955)
Emu, Remember! (1956)
The Crafte So Longe to Lerne (1959)
Poems for All the Annettes (1962)
The Blur in Between (1963)
The Cariboo Horses (1965)
North of Summer (1967)
Wild Grape Wine (1968)
The New Romans–Editor (1968)
Fifteen Winds (1969)
The Quest for Ouzo (1970)
Storm Warning–Editor (1970)
Love in a Burning Building (1970)
Selected Poems (1972)
Sex and Death (1973)
In Search of Owen Roblin (1974)
The Poems of Al Purdy (1976)
Storm Warning 2–Editor (1976)
Sundance at Dusk (1976)

Contents

Acknowledgements

All of the articles in this collection have been revised and updated for their appearance in this book. In their original forms they were published in the following periodicals: "Introduction: The Cartography of Myself," *Maclean's*, 1971; "The Iron Road," *Canada Month*, 1963; "Lights on the Sea: Portraits of BC Fishermen," *Maclean's*, 1974; "Cougar Hunter," *Weekend*, 1974; "Malcolm Lowry," The Montreal *Gazette*, 1974; "Imagine a Town," unpublished, written in 1972; "Dryland Country," *Canadian*, 1977; "Streetlights on the St. Lawrence," *Weekend*, 1974; "Angus," *Weekend*, 1974; "Norma, Eunice, and Judy," *Weekend*, 1974; "Seven-League Skates: A Talk with Brian Glennie," *Weekend*, 1975; "Poets in Montreal," originally written in 1970, *Northern Journey*, 1976; "Bon Jour," unpublished, written in 1977; "Aklavik on the Mackenzie River," unpublished, written in 1976; "Harbour Deep," *Canadian*, 1977; "Argus in Labrador," *Weekend*, 1975; and "Her Gates Both East and West," *Maclean's*, 1972.

AWP

No Other Country

Introduction:
The Cartography of Myself

In early summer, 1965, I was coasting along in a Nordair
DC8, bound for Frobisher Bay, Baffin Island. It was about 4
AM and most of the other passengers were asleep, but I was
peering from the window watching the small reflection of
our aeroplane skimming over the blue water and floating ice
of Frobisher Bay, several thousand feet down. Low hills on
either side of us were patched with snow, like jersey cows.
The water was so blue that the colour looked phony; the sun
had been up for about an hour.

Far beneath the noisy DC8, ice floes reeled away south.
Black-and-white Arctic hills surrounded us. This was the
first time I had been to the Arctic, and I was so excited that I
could hardly sit still. In Cuba, England, France, and other
countries I'd felt like a stranger: but here, I'd never left
home. And I thought what an odd feeling it was in a region
that most people think is desolate and alien. But I felt that
the Arctic was just a northern extension of southern Canada. Baffin Island:

> A club-shaped word
> a land most unlike Cathay and Paradise
> but a place the birds return to
> a name I've remember since childhood
> in the first books I read —

I have this same feeling of enjoyment, of being at home, all
over Canada. Maybe part of the reason comes from an earlier feeling of being trapped forever in the town of Trenton,
Ontario, when I was a child: then the tremendous sense of
release when I escaped, riding the freight trains west during
the Depression. Also, I take a double view of history, for
then and now merge somewhat in my mind. Winnipeg is
also Fort Garry and Seven Oaks. Adolphustown, not far
from where I live in Prince Edward County, is the spot

where the United Empire Loyalists landed nearly 200 years ago. The restored fortress of Louisbourg in Cape Breton makes me feel like a living ghost, especially when looking at the tombstone of Captain Israel Newton who died there, a member of the colonial army from New England. And driving along the Don Valley Parkway, I think of the old Indian trails that take the same route under black asphalt. In cities everywhere, grass tries to push aside the concrete barriers of sidewalks.

I think especially of people in connection with places. Working on a highway near Penticton, British Columbia, with a fellow wanderer named Jim, shovelling gravel atop boiling tar: a speeding car ignored warning signs and nearly killed us; the big road foreman blistered that driver's hide until his face turned dull red.

And walking through the Okanagan Valley with my friend, picking cherries from orchards for food, sleeping wherever we could: sometimes in vacant sheds, and once buried in the pungent shavings of a sawmill. Then going to work for two weeks on a mountain farm, for a man whose name sounded like "Skimmerhorn." I got five dollars for those two weeks, cutting down trees with Jim and splitting them with wedges. At night, we listened to John McCormack sing "The Far Away Bells Are Ringing" on a wind-up phonograph. Jim stayed behind to work for a stake, but I gave up and rode the freights west to Vancouver. I never saw him again.

One of my favourite Canadian places is the area around Hazelton and Woodcock on the big bend of the Skeena River in British Columbia. I was stationed at Woodcock in 1943, helping to build a landing field as part of the defences for an expected Japanese invasion. Snow-covered mountains surrounded the barracks sheds, with the Skeena River racing down the green valley on its way to Prince Rupert. Sometimes there were eagles, circling overhead nearly as high as the sun. And on weekend passes, airmen from the base would hop freight trains to Hazelton or Smithers to drink beer and terrorize pleasurably the local female population.

In 1960 I went back to the big bend of the Skeena to do some writing about the Tsimshian Indians around Hazelton and Kispiox. I was driving a '48 Pontiac that coughed its way up and down the mountain roads, threatening to expire at any minute. But I managed to reach Kispiox on the Indian reservation, with its carved house fronts and rotting totem poles. The place seemed entirely deserted, so I drove past the village and down to the Kispiox River. Standing in the shallows, wearing hip waders and baseball caps, were some twenty American fishermen with station wagons parked nearby.

There are other places stored on my mind's memory tapes. Places where I feel comfortable, at home: the battle-field at Batoche, in Saskatchewan, where I camped in a trail-er; the highline tracks of the CPR near Field, BC, where I'd walked after a cop kicked me off a freight at Golden, then became a CPR labourer on a landslide blocking passage east for forty-eight hours, then rode in legal luxury to Calgary on a work train. And once there was a mile-long Arctic island, my home for three weeks of summer: I lay with my ear flat against the monstrous stone silence of the island, listening to the deep core of the world – silence unending and elemen-tal, leaked from a billion-year period before and after the season of man.

I think back to all the places I've been, the people I've met and the things I've done. Having written and edited some twenty books, I hope to write a dozen more – to follow all the unknown roads I have not explored, until they branch off and become other roads in my mind. . . .

There is a map in my head that I've carried there ever since I left school, and I connect it, oddly, with Leo Tolstoy. He wrote a short story called "How Much Land Does a Man Need," in which a man was given title, free and clear, to as much land as he could encircle on foot between sunup and sundown. The man was too greedy for land, tried to walk around too much of it, and died of exhaustion just before the sun went down.

But I have as much land as I need right now. There is a

tireless runner in my blood that encircles the borderlands of Canada through the night hours, and sleeps when day arrives. Then my mind awakes and the race continues. West with the long and lamentably undefended American border; north along the jagged British Columbia coast to the whale-coloured Beaufort Sea and the Arctic Islands; south again past Baffin and Newfoundland to the Maritimes and sea lands of the Grand Banks. This is the map of myself, what I was and what I became. It is a cartography of feeling and sensibility: and I think the man who is not affected at all by this map of himself that is his country of origin, that man is emotionally crippled.

My own country seems to me not aggressive, nor in search of war or conquest of any kind. It is exploring the broken calm of its domestic affairs. Slowly it investigates its own somewhat backward technology, and sets up committees on how not to do what for whom. My country is trying to resolve the internal contradictions of the Indian and French-Canadian nations it contains. In rather bewildered and stupid fashion it stared myopically at the United States, unable to assess the danger to the south – a danger that continually changes in economic character, and finally confronts us from within our own borders.

This is the map of my country, the cartography of myself.

Al Purdy
August, 1977

The Iron Road

Riding the boxcars out of Winnipeg in a
morning after rain so close to
the violent sway of fields it's
like running and running
naked with summer in your mouth
being a boy scarcely a moment and you
hear the rumbling iron roadbed singing
under the wheels at night and a door jerking open
mile after dusty mile riding into Regina with
the dust storm crowding behind you
night and morning over the clicking rails

The year was 1937, and I was seventeen. I rode the freight trains to Vancouver, along with thousands of other Canadians during the Great Depression. In the Hungry Thirties it seemed that half the population was on the move. The unemployed workmen of Toronto and Montreal and all the other big cities swarmed over the boxcars, moving west to the Prairies, west to Vancouver, wherever there might be hope of finding work.

There were also the professional hoboes, who always went in the opposite direction from where there was any rumour of employment. They lived in hobo jungles beside rivers and near the towns, never far from the railway yards. There they lit campfires, cooked food, washed clothing – if it was absolutely necessary – and told tales of the steel high-ways while standing over the fires at night. Of towns where housewives always invited you inside for dinner when you asked for a handout, and never handed you an axe while pointing sternly at the woodpile. Of towns where you never had to work, there was always plenty of beer . . . . But after a day or two in the jungle they got restless again, and boarded the train to Anywhere.

It was a dark night in early June when I caught my first train at the railway yards in Trenton, Ontario. It had chuffed in from the east an hour earlier, and was about to pull out for Toronto. The yards were full of shunting switch engines bustling back and forth in the night, red and green signal lights gleaming like the eyes of stationary cats, and every now and then you heard a hoarse, impatient scream from the whistles of the westbound train.

I'll never know how I had the nerve to board that train, for I was scared to death of it. I'd quit school a couple of years before, and there was no work at all in Trenton. But that wasn't the reason why I was heading west. The reason was boredom. I wanted adventure. That was why I crouched in some bushes beside the tracks, almost too nervous to breathe, wondering how I'd ever manage to climb onto that boxcar. Was it something like getting on a bicycle or a horse? And where were the railway police hiding?

Suddenly the westbound train made a peculiar "toot-toot" that signaled departure – a sound I've heard many times since. Hoboes call it "the highball." Then a great met-allic crash came from the couplings, and the train grunted away into the night. I broke from cover and ran alongside, grabbing at the steel ladder of a passing boxcar, and climbed up onto the roof—collapsing on the swaying catwalk while all the vertebrae of the wriggling wooden serpent beneath me thundered west.

A few days later and miles from home, I received my first instructions from a professional bum about the proper method of boarding a moving train. A lean little man with a dark stubble of beard, he'd seen me swing onto a train by the rear ladder of a boxcar.

"That's the way guys get killed," he said. "Ya gotta do it the right way." He spat tobacco on the boxcar floor and gestured. "I seen guys lose a leg or arm falling under them wheels. Ya always go for the ladder at the front end of the car, never the one at the back end. If ya miss yer hold on the rear ladder ya fall between the cars and yer a gone goose. Always the front ladder. An remember that, kid."

There were other famous bums who wrote their names and deeds on boxcar walls or on the supports of watertanks with knife and pencil—Regina Sam Jones, Montana Slim, Midnight Frank. I've often wondered: why should a man call himself "Midnight Frank"? There was also the immortal Kilroy, who wrote "Kilroy was here" the length and breadth of the continent.

Farther west, at Broadview, Saskatchewan, the Mounties had a reputation for being very tough on bums. The stories about their toughness alarmed me so much that I crawled down the trap door of a threshing machine mounted on a flatcar before going through town. I crouched in the darkness of that monster, nervously waiting to be discovered and hauled off to jail. I heard the police tramping around outside, making a tremendous racket, but they didn't find me. When the train pulled out on its way west, I was the only illicit passenger left of the three score or so who had ridden with me into Broadview.

When I first started out for Vancouver I had some money in my pockets. But it was soon spent. I had to forsake the aristocratic habit of eating in restaurants and join the other bums knocking on doors to ask for handouts. It was embarrassing, but I got used to it. You nerved yourself, knocked on a door, and waited, wondering what might happen. The dignity of man was, of course, a lesser consideration than being hungry.

You might get a sandwich from a housewife, perhaps even a full meal, a "sitdown" we used to call it; but you might also be given an axe and directed to the woodpile; or a man in shirtsleeves might come to the door and tell you to "Beat it, bum!" It was all part of the game, and you didn't really hold any grudges for a harsh reception. You just kept on trying.

Sometimes you went to the bakery of whatever small town you happened to be passing through, asking the baker if he had any stale bread or buns. Most of the time you got something to eat, but occasionally there were long stretches on the train where it wasn't possible to ask for a handout. At such times you stayed hungry.

On my first trip west I hitchhiked north from Sault Ste. Marie, and was disheartened to find that the road ended at a little village called Searchmont (at that time the Trans-Canada Highway was not yet completed through Northern Ontario). Near midnight I boarded a freight travelling north and west, riding in an open-air gondola used to transport coal. After an hour it began to rain, and the coaldust made things worse. My face and hands were streaked with it. We stopped around 5 AM and it was still dark. I had no idea where I was, but the rain and coaldust were too miserable to be borne. I ripped the seal off a boxcar with my hunting knife and tried to get inside. But the door was too big and heavy for me to move, so I went back to my gondola and huddled under the rain in silent misery.

A railway cop materialized out of the greyness not long after I got settled. He'd seen the broken seal, and knew I was responsible. He told me that the settlement was named Hawk Junction, then locked me up in a caboose with barred windows and padlocked door. And I thought: how would my mother feel now about her darling boy? At noon the railway cop took me to his house for dinner with his wife and children, gave me some *Ladies Home Journals* to read, and casually mentioned that I could get two years for breaking the boxcar seal.

When returned to my prison-on-wheels I felt panicstricken. I was only seventeen, and this was the first time I'd ventured far away from home. I examined the caboose-prison closely, thinking: two years! Why, I'd be nineteen when I got out, an old man! And of course it was hopeless to think of escape. Other prisoners had tried without success, and windows were broken where they'd tried to wrench out the bars. And the door: it was wood, locked on the outside with a padlock, opening inward. It was a very springy door though: I could squeeze my fingertips between sill and door, one hand at the top and the other a foot below. That gave me hope, blessed hope, for the first time. My six-foot-three body was suspended in air by my hands, doubled up like a coiled spring, and I pulled. Lord, how I pulled! The door bent inward until I could see a couple of daylight inches between door and sill. Then, Snap! and screws pulled out of the steel hasp outside. I fell flat on my back.

Peering cautiously outside, right and left, I jumped to the ground, walking as slowly and sedately as I could make myself – toward freedom. The urge to run was hard to resist, especially when crossing a bridge over a wide river along the tracks, and continuing steadily in the direction of Sault Ste. Marie, 165 miles south of the railway divisional point. But that cop would be looking for me, and so would other blue uniforms! Two years! Walking the tracks would make me far too obvious, much too easy to find. So how about making the journey twenty or thirty feet into the heavy forest lining both sides of the right of way? That way I could see if anyone came after me, and duck back among the trees. Brilliant, positively brilliant.

But the trees went uphill and down, turned leftways and rightways, without landmarks or anything to orient me with the tracks. I began to feel uneasy: better stay close to the railway. Too late. I was deep into the woods, not knowing in which direction to turn. I was lost – and didn't even feel stupid, just terrified. My heart began to pump hard, and I ran, with branches and leaves slapping my face, blundering into trees, splashing through little streams.

Finally I stopped, knowing panic was useless but feeling it anyway. The possibility of dangerous animals occurred to me: what about bears?—bears must live in these woods. I had no defense against them; the railway cop had confiscated my hunting knife. Besides, what good would such a feeble weapon be against an angry black bear? And the brown shape that flitted between the trees, not so much seen as realized, what was that?

I slept on the side of a hill, huddled around a mother-tree, and it was cold, cold. Morning was grey with a light rain falling, more mist than rain. By this time I'd thought of the sun as some kind of directional reference, but there was no sun. And just a couple of miles away I could hear engines shunting and butting back and forth in the railway yard, the sound seeming to come from all directions among the trees. Old logging trails meandered through the forest, but they were so old that when I tried to follow them they vanished in the vague greyness. Once I stumbled on an old hunting camp, so ancient that the lean-to logs were rotten. Later in the day, during my stumbling, lurching progress, I came on that hunting camp twice more, each time increasingly terrified about walking in circles.

At age seventeen I didn't believe in God, at least I told myself I didn't. But this was no time to take chances one way or the other. I prayed. Fervently, passionately, and with no reservations, I prayed to get out of that forest. And remembered the forty-some Sundays I'd attended church two years before, without listening to the preacher's sermon but in order to receive a prize for attendance. Since then I'd become a non-believer in that fire-and-brimstone God, but now for reasons of expediency I pretended to myself and to a possible Him that my backsliding was over—at least for as long as I was lost in this northern forest.

And maybe it worked: I still don't know. That railway bridge I'd crossed when leaving Hawk Junction popped into my head. Adolescent high school logic took over. The river and railway tracks would make two sides of a very large iso-sceles triangle. And carry it a step farther: if I could finally walk in something close to a straight line, which hadn't happened thus far, then I must finally locate either river or tracks. And the sun, now becoming a pale spot in the overhead grey, gave me some small direction. I walked and walked, and two hours later nearly fell head-first down an embankment into that blessed blessed river.

That same evening I boarded a passenger train just behind the engine, and rode south to the Soo in style, careless of legal consequences. But no cops appeared on the smoky, cindered horizon of fear. At the steel town I dived into a Scandinavian steambath to stop the shivering chill that I'd picked up from two days in the woods. And sleeping that night in a cheap flophouse, I was still shuddering a little, in slow motion.

I think my first sight of the mountains was worth all the hardships – waking early in the morning inside an empty boxcar and gazing down into a lake surrounded by forest stretching for miles and miles – cupped and cradled by the white peaks. And myself crawling round the side of a mountain like a fly on a sugar bowl. For the first time I realized how big this country was. And, naively, because I was only seventeen years old, I felt a tremendous exaltation at the sight. How marvelous to be alive and to ride a bare-backed train through such a country. And, naively, forty years later, I've not changed my mind.

Vancouver was a sprawling, dingy, beautiful giant of a waterfront city even in 1937. I walked down Water Street, over the puddles and wet grey concrete in the early morning. An old Indian woman on an iron balcony called down for me to come up and see her daughter, mentioning explicitly certain delights that could be expected. Rather prudishly, I declined. I spent the afternoon at a movie, paying fifteen cents for the privilege of watching Dorothy Lamour disport herself in a sarong. But I'm not sure if the Indian girl wouldn't have been a better bargain.

After the movie I was seized with a realization of the immense distance I had come from home. Originally I had meant to get a job fishing on a purse seiner at Vancouver, but the smelly old harbour depressed me. The Lions Gate Bridge, stretching spider-like across First Narrows, seemed alien; the streets themselves were unfriendly and peopled by strangers. I was homesick.

On the same day that I had arrived I slipped under the barrier at a level crossing and boarded a freight train moving east. And all the immense width of a continent was before me again, all the lakes and rivers and mountains—and the green country of childhood lay behind.

Riding into the Crowsnest mountains with
your first beard itching and a
hundred hungry guys fanning out thru
the shabby whistlestops for handouts and
not even a sandwich for two hundred miles
only the high mountains and knowing
what it's like to be not quite a child
any more and listening to the tough men
talk of women and talk of the way things are
in 1937—

Lights on the Sea:
Portraits of BC Fishermen

In 1937 when I rode the freight trains west, I had intended to get a job on the fishing boats in Vancouver; but homesickness forced me to hop on an eastbound train on the very day of my arrival in Vancouver–without ever having tried to get a job on a fishing boat. I was seventeen.

Thirty-seven years later I rode a seiner fish packer west from Vancouver harbour at midnight. Enjoying myself thoroughly, standing with feet wide apart on the gently heaving steel deck, deciding that even if I'd written the script I couldn't have made things more dramatic: Vancouver lights all pointing toward the ship and myself, neon arrows on the black water; the packer, *Pacific Ocean*, a momentary centre of the universe. Red and white lights all around, Stanley Park a dark animal crouched low in water. Slipping under the Lions Gate Bridge, with soundless cars passing 200 feet over our heads and a white moon some 200,000 miles farther up. Ernie, the cook, is at the rail playing his harmonica–the Toreador song from *Carmen*, I think.

In the wheelhouse Skipper Herb Shannon, a veteran of fifty years at sea, steers the packer toward Juan de Fuca Strait. (In the last century Herb's father sailed wind ships across the Pacific.) Herb Shannon, a little man in baggy khaki pants, reminds me of a retired railway engineer (nobody ever looks like what they are); he talks about fishing while the boat rolls queasily and I wonder about that last dish of blueberries at dinner.

"Well," I say, because I can't think of anything else, "how does your wife like you being late for almost all your meals?"

"She knew what I was doin' before I married her," he says. And behind us the blaze of lights is growing dim.

On a packer, two hours out from Vancouver, the transmitted motion of the sea is not the same rocking-chair dream it is at the Fraser's mouth. Dub, the engineer and half-owner of the boat, says, "You look kinda green." I hold onto cables at port or starboard, trying to keep my eyes on some fixed object, according to previous advice. There is no getting away from it, I am not a well man. Water slops over the rail with each sickening heave. At this point I lose a plate of blueberries right off the top of my stomach. I have not been so sick in all my damn life. Ernie plays the harmonica unfeelingly. I am dying.

At 3:30 AM we strike a floating field of logs in Active Pass, thirty miles or so southwest of Victoria. Motors stop, we drift among the logs on the sea's momentum alone, bumping gently toward clear water. Herb Shannon, in the wheelhouse, guiding us to safety. Sunk in near-death unconsciousness in my quarters, I do not even lift my head from the bunk after we strike. Next day in the galley:

"Fine sailor you are," Dub says.

And Herb Shannon, sipping hot coffee: "You'll get used to it."

I'd better.

The area around here, north of Cape Flattery and along the southwest coast of Vancouver Island, is "the graveyard of the Pacific," thus named for good and sufficient reasons.

The Japanese Current drives north along the American coast; eastbound ships get careless and don't watch their radar sometimes. Only eighteen months ago a Japanese ship with a cargo of Dodge Colt automobiles wrecked on the southwest coast of Vancouver Island, a few miles north. It's still there, stranded among rocks like great stone teeth.

"Of course, those Colt curb-jumpers disappeared damn quick," Herb Shannon says. "Miraculous the way things disappear off a wrecked ship. Barges pulled alongside and the cars got winched off. . . ."

At Port Renfrew, a fine deep-sea harbour on Vancouver Island's west coast, seiners and gill-netters march toward us through the early morning mist—*Sun Burst, Sherry Joan, Sea Fair, Silver Luck, Joyce R.,* and *Georgia Saga.* Most of them come directly from the "surf-line" boundaries, established by a 1957 unwritten agreement between the United States and Canada that no salmon fishing with nets will be allowed beyond the surf-line. The agreement covers the coasts of California, Oregon, Washington, Alaska, and British Columbia. Its purpose is to conserve the salmon stock for each country, although the Canadian fishermen say that the United States almost invariably takes the eagle's share of salmon bound for spawning grounds on BC rivers. One reason for the disproportionately larger American catch is that, after the agreement was made, Alaska decided its fishing area would extend three miles seaward from the surf-line that had been established for the other coastal states and British Columbia. One might call this an international doublecross, but Canadian fisheries officials are rarely that impolite.

Now, this situation makes a lot of BC fishermen pretty resentful. One hears talk of blockading the Fraser's mouth with nets and simply cleaning it out of fish. But that is obviously self-defeating, for 15 to 20 per cent of salmon must reach their home waters in the Fraser and its tributaries to spawn. If they were blockaded, the rich ocean harvest of the great river would vanish entirely. The only rational answer is further arbitration and agreement through the International Pacific Salmon Fisheries Commission.

High Rose, Brilon, and *Miss Jennie* swing bow and stern expertly alongside the *Pacific Ocean,* skippers joshing good-naturedly with the packer's crew. "Who's the city man?" Joe LePore wants to know, meaning me, of course.

LePore says he hates fishing, wants to quit. "Too many boats working here; you can't catch enough fish. But with a family, how can I quit?"

Rosemary Wilson, a fisherman's widow with no children, is alone on the gill-netter. "Why?" I ask her. She chuckles deep inside her windbreaker.

"There's more fish at sea than men ashore." Which is fair enough, but near the season's end there aren't enough fish, either.

The *Pacific Ocean* leaves Port Renfrew on a fish-pick-up trip to Sooke, some forty miles south. We move directly into the northward-driving Japanese Current, with a sneaky twisting slop striking us from the west, as well. Hastily I swallow seasickness pills, with a despairing look at Herb Shannon. Too late. Already my whole body feels like Lazarus seven days dead, arms and legs almost useless, brain active but hardly helpful. And watching a fixed object on the horizon doesn't work at all. I take to my bunk, holding onto the high varnished sides desperately, afraid that I might survive.

I try to think of something else besides my sick sick self. Albert Radil, for instance. I met him on the BC Packers' dock at Steveston. He's one of the fishermen's aristocracy. By contrast to Radil, gill-netters and seiners probably averaged $5,000 to $6,000 a year in 1971; whereas Radil's boat, the *Royal Canadian,* cost half a million to build, and his catch is correspondingly valuable. He isn't wealthy, in the same overwhelming sense as are people like E.P. Taylor and the Bronfmans: but his wealth takes the form of achievement—being a high-liner and among the top fishermen every year, being the man who comes to mind immediately when one thinks of the best.

Albert Radil is a nondescript, red-faced middle-aged man in a faded checked shirt and work trousers. He's mild-mannered and far-distant from the image of Jack London's savage tyrant skippers. Unloading a ten-day record of ground fish – turbot, cod, sole, and ocean perch, caught by dragging long nylon nets over the sea bottom – Albert and his five-man crew have dumped 387,000 pounds of rainbow cargo into the black hold of the 105-foot *Royal Canadian*. Of course, ground fish fetch only five cents a pound, except for sole, which are ten cents. But the total value of that catch comes to around twenty thousand dollars.

What I want to know from Albert is exactly why he is such a good fisherman. He says it's because of all the ship's electronic equipment – sonar, echo sounders, net monitors, Loran radio, as well as the nearly standard radar; also, the ability to use them to advantage. Which isn't what I mean. Other draggers besides the *Royal Canadian* have the same slick devices, uncanny robot marvels that map the ocean bottom, actually outlining schools of fish – and even single lone-wolf fish – on paper in the wheelhouse.

I think Albert is slightly bewildered by the fact that I prefer any other explanation besides the wealth of equipment and his own long experience. He knows he's a highliner, is modest about it, and long years at the job enable him to fish where the fish are, and to use all the technological gimmicks as if they were familiar and trusted extensions of his own mind. But I am trying to make something intangible become visible – maybe some ability that he isn't aware of himself.

John Radil, Albert's eighty-year-old father, born in Yugoslavia, speech thickened by old age and remote traces of the sea-fringed Balkans, accompanies us around the boat. Albert says, "His life, you know. He's been a fisherman since he was a small boy, can't stay away even now." I look at the old man with respect, but can't understand his geriatric language.

Behind us, the crew is unloading tons and tons of varicoloured fish, winches humming, scrape and curse of metal on metal, buzz of words: and I'm still intrigued by Albert, the unassuming but confident man-of-the-sea, with a golden touch, with the admiration of everyone I talk to about him. . . .

"All right, then," I say, still trying to find the secret of expertise, "how do you know where to go to find those fish in the first place?"

Is there pity for my obtuseness in Albert's eyes? "We follow the edge of the banks," he says. "That's where the fish find their food." He means those undersea plateaus that are the rich feeding grounds of all west-coast fish. And he shows me their location on the wheelhouse charts, depths noted, rocks that might destroy nets marked, everything seemingly organized by an electronic file clerk in the computer of the human mind.

My own mind can see him there, dragging the seas south of the Queen Charlottes with his immense net, wind blowing and the water choppy, greenish light from the wheelhouse radar deepening the lines in his face, waterproof brain thrusting below the surface to follow contours of deep-down feeding grounds, answering light in his eyes flashing acknowledgement of the machines' flow of information, all the various streams of experience and intuition coming together in a nearly magical kind of awareness.

"Knowledge and experience," Albert says again. Then he introduces me to Bob Giljuich, who once walked on the backs of fish at the fifteen-foot-wide net mouth while it was being reeled inboard.

"Walked on the water?" I want to know, having some weird vision of Christ on Galilee, I suppose. Giljuich, a rawboned youngster with projecting extremities, says no.

"There was so many fish in the net it was like they was solid, like on the ground almost."

Bob Giljuich goes back to work unloading fish. And I see that these pragmatic men are not going to give me any kind of mystical explanations. The radar, which Albert has switched on for my benefit, sweeps its circular light around under glass, outlining Vancouver Island, miles away across the Gulf of Georgia. He nods at me. That is how it is done. All right.

Once the *Pacific Ocean* is back at Port Renfrew the seasickness is gone, leaving me with the conviction that I'm a confirmed landsman. In mid-afternoon a Cessna 180 lands a few hundred yards from the *Pacific Ocean*. It's taking me to Tofino, along the west coast of British Columbia. Pilot: Bobby Wingham, manager of Canfisco at Tofino. And there's nothing to make the flesh feel so vulnerable as these flying baby carriages, powered by twisted rubberbands. Farther north along the coast we spot that wrecked Japanese freighter, now shorn of its automotive cargo, creamy waves lapping its sides. The pilot glances at me sideways, perhaps meaning to be reassuring. I hold onto the handle dingus installed for nervous passengers. Am I nervous, am I reassured? Yes. And no.

Tofino is a fishing village with one main street, two groceries, and a hotel. Its location might be described as west of nowhere: but nowhere has miles and miles of white sand beaches, sounding whales off the blue lace-fringed sea's edge if you're lucky enough to see them, and maybe 300 trollers growing like a watery forest from the harbour. Trollers because the surf-line agreement prohibits net fishing for salmon. And a scarcely touched primeval paradise all around the village.

But Tofino for me is mostly Gil Sadler. He's a troller, age thirty-three, ex-carpenter, married with kids and owns his own house – kind of a gee-whiz, gosh-all-fishhooks sort of guy. I mean the fortunate kind who strikes you as partly a kid still, even though physically a man. Five years ago Sadler decided to be a fisherman, despite the more than 6,000 licensed fishing boats operating in British Columbia. He did some soul-searching about it with his wife, bought an elderly thirty-six-foot troller, and renovated her, calling her the *Promisewell* since fishing seemed to promise a better life for his family.

But here was the rub: Sadler had never fished before in his life, except with hook and worms off the dock. Then what about Joe McLeod, the brash, confident record-setter and pacemaker for all the local fishermen? No doubt the fish were actually afraid not to bite his hooks, or else McLeod might speak to God about it. Gil Sadler knew McLeod slightly, and was sure of help from him. And he got it, too, but not exactly as expected. He described himself sailing the *Promisewell*, to McLeod, following the edge of a shoal feeding ground where salmon ought to be, should be, *must* be feeding, and using a particular kind of bait. McLeod would grunt enigmatically and say of that, "Should be a different colour!" To which Sadler would respond eagerly, face lighting up at a word from the master, "What kind of bait do you think is best, Mr. McLeod?"

But McLeod never gave him a direct answer, letting the younger man figure it out for himself, dropping tantalizing hints on where and how and when things should be done. The old master fisherman, kindly but not too kindly, wise but not relinquishing his hard-won wisdom too easily so that someone who hadn't earned it over the hard experience of years could pick it up and profit by it. But kindly, nevertheless. How could one *not* respond to such open admiration for himself in the fresh-faced young fisherman?

Gil rode the elderly *Promisewell* into the open Pacific, fishing with spoons and butterflies sometimes, the colour of the lures changed to match changing colour of the water. High winds blowing, hurricanes lifting knouts of swirling water in columns out of the frantic, whip-lashed sea. And running – sometimes running like a scared fool – in hundred-mile-an-hour winds for the safety of a little opening in the rocky shore, a cove like the Biblical house of refuge. And twelve-foot sheets of water ripped from the sea's face, rigging literally torn off the boat like clothes from a scarecrow, leaving only the stripped-down hull.

Once in a fog in a dream, a 300-foot Russian trawler loomed over the *Promisewell*, and the little boat quivered with fear. The trawler's whistle blew deafeningly, continuously. But which way was the damn thing going? Is that the bow I'm looking at or the stern? What shall I do, what would Joe McLeod have done? Then, what use my eight measly trolling lines against this giant floating claw that snatches whole schools and tribes of fish from the sea? Only the comparatively high price for fish caught with hook and line—ranging at that time from $1.40 to $2.15 a pound for coho and spring salmon—made it worthwhile; and the desperate drive toward excellence, as well,—excellence embodied by Joe McLeod.

Listen to other fishermen on the radio: voices talking without bodies on the solitary sun-blinded sea. Now the Loran radio signal whispers; match that with a corresponding number on the chart where shoals and fish are waiting! How long will the fish wait? You're there, all eight lines out, trolling the bank: rush back into the wheelhouse to check the Loran, check the echo sounder for fish, glance at the depth finder and all those little flashing lights and sounds connected with electrodes fixed in a human brain.

And salmon, their long gleaming silver bodies flopping out of the sea, coho transformed into dollar bills and groceries; spring salmon become a new room built onto the house, mortgage paid off, desperate anxiety about being a loser changed to the elation of a winner. Then laughter? Amusement at one's self, the half-phony laughter soon silent when salmon disappear, fading to nothing but the blood's whisper and murmur of your own breathing, defeated sound of feet scuffing a worn deck slippery with fish scales.

But riding home to Tofino in the elderly *Promisewell* with 1,700 salmon—stern awash, deck awash, bow juddering and trembling from the engine's feeble efforts, the whole worn-out Rube-Goldberg contraption not quite sinking—veteran fisherman mutter, "Throw some o' them fish back, boy, or you'll never make it to hum, boy!"

Under your breath: "Well, old boys, I'm making it, somehow, home!" After which a new record is weighed and counted for one years' fishing out of Tofino, the cash value: $18,500.

And weaving a little with good tiredness up the town's main drag, clothes covered with blood and fish slime, covered with dirty glorious triumph. And the woman seeing you at the house door, knowing it all from the look on your face, how the uncertainty ends in you as it ends in her.

And Joe McLeod? But, of course, McLeod will be pleased, happy you've learned what you had to learn, and the dollar bills stacked in one corner of his mind will move aside, allowing generosity and fellowship to take over.

Lights at the Co-op Grocery come on, people inside moving toward the cashier's counter. Sun dimming beyond green pop-up hills and clustered familiar islands. Home is a warm blanket all around, an order of priorities for everything known and established, friends waiting to say "Well done!" and shake your hand. It's almost too much, or nearly too little, like a picture on the living room wall that says, smugly, "God Bless Our Home" and has to be straightened after the kids knock it sideways playing inside on a rainy day. Sadler laughs softly, walking toward Joe McLeod's house in Tofino. A woman with a brown bag of groceries cradled in one arm looks at him, thoughts elsewhere from her eyes, and moves on toward her different destinations.

The stone backside of Canada is not the mainland Coast Range, but the savage bare peaks of Vancouver Island, surrounded by forests nearly as inaccessible as another planet. Riding a different Cessna 180 we swing over them, eastbound for a fish cannery at Namu, about 180 miles south of Prince Rupert. Again this feeling of being stranded in mid-air, hanging onto a wriggling piece of two-by-four. Below us the lumbering town of Gold River belches anal dregs into the sky. I think of ex-Premier Bennett's comforting words: "I like the smell of pollution, it's the smell of progress!" In which case we have a lot of progress here. Whole mountains stripped of timber in a wilderness so vast it seems that the last green tree could never be destroyed. But we're trying.

We lift over the BC Inland Passage to Alaska, uninhabited green islands "more a kingdom than a province" – high half-frozen lakes feeding their overflow to other lakes farther down the mountains, then still other lakes in shimmering necklaces strung together on top of the world. And fishing boats far below are water-beetles, their mile-long wakes reduced to seeming inches. Then Namu, a four-million-dollar cannery with its machinery silent and only the refrigeration plant in operation.

It's country so beautiful that nobody deserves to die without having seen it. Bald eagles fly over the bunkhouses; salmon throng in the harbour, unable to ascend the low-water river until the next rainfall. Raised boardwalks wind through the trees, connecting bunkhouses, cannery, refrigeration plant, and deserted Japanese village nestled at the edge of the rain forest. A BC Packers' company town in 1971, it employs only about eighty people instead of the 500 it carried in its heyday years ago.

Fishermen–gill-netters and seiners by scores–swarm around the floating docks–Indian, Japanese, and various breeds of Europeans now become Canadian. Everyone has a non-urgent air about them, no hurry to do anything, for the best fishing is over. But Indian kids make long casts with bare hooks into the harbour, and snag a fat coho when their luck runs good. Carlo Politano lounges on his boat, dark, heavy-set, big nose dominating his features. Carlo is sixty-three now, and thirty-six years a fisherman. He started years ago because of owing $360, and paid that debt in his second year. It's a lonely job now, for all his friends are gone.

"In the old days you'd see a boat chimney smoking, and three or four guys would row over for coffee or rum or breakfast." A sadness shades his thickening face. "I can't take the rough weather any more."

On a float nearby, two Indian girls work skilfully to repair nets: Ena and Lorna, who make $3.60 an hour.

"Good girls," Carlo says. "They're invited to white people's houses."

Les Brown is sixtyish, brown from sun and sea, shop steward at the refrigeration plant. "Workers at Namu average about three dollars an hour and pay sixty dollars a week for room and board at the bunkhouse," he tells me. Scott worked at a whaling station owned by BC packers on Vancouver Island in the early fifties, introduced a union there, and lost his job. Now, ironically, he works for the same company at Namu.

Alonzo McGarvie, gill-netter and dangerous-tempered ex-fighter, was said to have knocked five men cold when they attacked him one memorable night for allegedly stealing their fish. I saw him as we left Namu, weaving along the dock and swinging a case of beer, with a bottle of whisky sticking out of his pocket.

We're riding the supply boat, *Canadian Number One*, north from Namu to Bella Bella and Klemtu before we head back to Vancouver. George Radil, son of Albert, the son of John, is wearing carpet slippers and steering expertly with his feet. On the starboard side of the boat a humpback whale blows and dives. When we reach Bella Bella a dozen Indian young-sters swarm over the boat. If the crew hadn't shooed them away, they might have sailed away to a south sea island.

Back in Vancouver, Barry McMillin, brisk young manager of J.S. McMillin Fisheries, says that his small company (six million dollars gross sales a year – is that small?) is more efficient and has less overhead than the bigger ones. "Besides, we don't have the ill-will that those big companies sometimes generate." McMillin owns three boats and con-tracts six more. He estimates that the four-man crew of a dragger can make up to $30,000 per person per season. And adds, "Give us an even break, and we'll beat the big boys every time."

John Wolff is a halibut long-liner out of Vancouver, seventy years old and looking about fifty-five, black hair only slightly sprinkled with grey. He has fished all his life and doesn't expect to spend the rest of it any differently. His hal-ibut long-liner operates north of Banks Island in Hecate Strait, the halibut feeding grounds. (A long-liner is a 300-fa-thom-long cable to which are fastened short lines for bot-tom fishing.) Wolff talks about a time when a pod of 150 killer whales was on both sides and behind the long-liner.

"When whales blow they smell awful bad, and it was like being in the middle of a big garbage dump. Most of them had their mouths open. You could see their teeth. I was never so scared before or since."

Wolff thinks that Canada should have a fifty-mile continental limit, the same as Iceland. "Most fishermen I know feel the same. Just look at it this way," he says seriously. "Take the salmon and halibut; they're on their way to BC coastal rivers to spawn when we catch them, so in a manner of speaking we paid their board and lodging. It isn't right that other countries like Japan, Russia, and the United States should catch those fish."

At the Campbell Street wharf I meet Vance Fletcher, bearded tuna fishermen, long dark hair, age thirty. A slim, athletic animal in his movements, bubbling excitement held just under the surface of his talk. Fletcher operates a fifty-foot long-liner with a three-man crew, who've just returned after ten days out with a catch of more that $7,000 worth of tuna. But listening to him, all is not beer and skittles (or fish and chips?) in the fishing industry.

Cape Chacon, he explains, is a southern point in Alaska, three miles from the Canadian Nunez Rock. "Now, the International Boundary should run right in the middle of those two points, and it does. It *does*. And yet the Alaska Fisheries people claim a three-mile limit from Cape Chacon, which takes in the Canadian Nunez Rock. What it means is that our fishing boats are chased by American patrols in Canadian territorial waters." Fletcher's eyes flash a little. "Of course, we don't stop, but someone could get killed out there if the Americans get trigger-happy—as they are sometimes."

Fletcher lives and eats fishing; on this last trip he took a hundred tuna in forty-five minutes. And that's $600. "In the last few years I've been tryin' to get outa debt; before that I blew more than $150,000. What for? Well, maybe I wanted to regain the life I missed as a kid because of fishing." He says that a fisherman works on instincts and reflexes, and those make the difference between a good man and a bohunk. The *Island Queen*, his present boat, is six years old. The one before that went down in a storm in Hecate Strait. He says of himself, "They say I'm a legend in my own time." I wonder if he knows how he sounds.

From Norman Safarik on Fisherman's Wharf I hear of Anton Kowalski for the first time: an ex-soldier from the Polish army, a loner and a wild, unpredictable oddball. Kowalski operated a seventy-foot, one-man dragger ten years ago, always with a girl or two for company, and generally with a bottle whose contents he sampled freely. When the federal fisheries people were in process of seizing his boat for illegal halibut fishing, he revved the motors to full speed in reverse, broke his mooring lines and escaped into Vancouver harbour. Once in open water he threw all the halibut overboard by hand, thus providing no evidence of poaching—even though the uniformed officials watched the whole procedure with open mouths on shore.

Safarik, a fishing company owner, tells of Kowalski's boat going down in a storm twenty-five miles from Prince Rupert. "But he managed to get ashore with his girl in a skiff he'd borrowed from me. There were no oars; he'd forgotten to take them. The crazy bastard had to carve oars from driftwood and row all the way to Rupert in early winter." Safarik shakes his head in amazement. "After that he disappeared for a long time. Everyone thought he was dead. Then I got a phone call, and a kinda ghostly voice says he's Anton. 'But you're dead,' I tell him. 'Maybe so,' he says, 'but I got 20,000 pounds of rock sole to sell you before they bury me.' "

After screwballs like Kowalski it's no surprise to hear about another one, for British Columbia has more of these than any other province. The name Alvo von Alvensleben still evokes amazement, even if I can't pronounce it. A young immigrant, scion of German nobility, he came to British Columbia in 1904, married an Okanagan-peaches and Fraser-Valley-cream girl, and got involved in the fishing industry. In 1910 von Alvensleben built a cannery called "Pacofi" on Selwyn Inlet off Hecate Strait, using foreign money for its construction. Nothing unusual about that.

When World War I broke out, von Alvensleben disappeared for parts unknown with his Canadian wife. Pacofi, the cannery he left behind, went through several different owners, eventually winding up as the property of BC Packers in 1938. Its machinery being long out of date, the plant was torn down. Below the building were found mysterious and elaborate concrete installations, whose purpose puzzled the wreckers so much that measurements and pictures were taken. These were submitted to experts in structural design, who revealed that a submarine base had existed under the Pacofi cannery for twenty-eight years, right to the brink of World War II.

In the character of the fishermen I've met there is some quality I keep trying to define. Not something that will make a man stand out in a crowd, but more like a composite of Vance Fletcher's arrogant independence, the sturdy, undeviating lifestyle of John Wolff, and a wrapped-around loneliness that comes from driving their boats along the intricate, indented coastline of British Columbia in summer and winter, storm and calm.

Through these coastal wanderings, I've somehow caught up with some of my own life that should have been lived before. On my final trip, aboard a Canadian Fishing Company power launch, early-morning gill-netters at the Fraser River's mouth lower their 200-fathoms-long nylon nets like undersea fences into the grey-green water. These are manned by drowsy, half-awake men, and one by a woman. There's Roy Morimoto, born in Japan in 1920, come to Canada as a child, and moved east during the war with Japan, away from the vulnerable-to-sabotage Pacific coast; and George Woods, hauling his net aboard with the hydraulic gurdie, to remove—eleven crabs, one empty milk carton, and two salmon. "The way to make a living, boy," George says.

The floating town of gill-netters lifts lazily on the tide; we rock into daylight sleep. Just as I'm leaving, Roy Morimoto gives me a big silvery sockeye: and he caught only four all last night! The life I should have lived before has been lived for the first time—among people that I seem to have known for all my lives.

Cougar Hunter

Roderick Haig-Brown was a professional bounty hunter for cougars on northern Vancouver Island at age twenty-two, in the early 1930s. He told me about Cougar Smith, then the official predator hunter, when the price paid for a dead cougar was forty or fifty dollars. Smith was about fifty-eight, lean and spare as a lodgepole pine, generally with a roll-your-own smoke hanging from his lower lip. Dogs are always used to trail cougars, but sometimes, over logging slash on dry ground – such as on this occasion – the dogs are baffled and show no interest. So there's Cougar Smith following the trail himself, specs sagging low on his nose so he can peer over them, picking one cougar hair from a log, noticing faint paw prints on dusty ground, moving from one sign to another with a kind of informed intuition. And it's quite likely that there's a 200-pound cougar holed up for the day in heavy timber beyond the logged area, waiting for the prowling night.

There's something attractive and yet uncanny about this

woods runner and tracker, Cougar Smith. It brings to mind Dan'l Boone, also the fictional detective in *Les Misérables*, trailing his criminal through the sewers of Paris. Ridiculous, of course. But Cougar Smith's reputation had preceded him when he visited the Nimpkish River country to hunt with Haig-Brown. The young man, only a few years out from England, and the old bounty hunter roamed the woods companionably together, chasing the big cats.

Cougars, sometimes called "mountain lions," may reach nine feet in length. They can weigh up to 250 pounds. Their ordinary prey is the mountain deer population. But sometimes they become outlaws when old or crippled, and they kill sheep and cattle. The procedure then is for the farmer to get in touch with a professional hunter, who arrives on the scene with dogs. They bark and yap on the trail, generally treeing the cougar. And shortly thereafter the hunter arrives with his rifle. But cougars, grown old and wise, have been known to double back and forth across a river to confuse pursuers, refusing to be treed, occasionally turning on tormenting dogs to kill them with one swipe of a powerful paw. They kill deer in much the same way, leaping on the terrified animal's back, reaching around with one paw under its nose, and wrenching backward and up to break the gentle creature's neck.

And yet they are valuable and beautiful and fascinating to watch. I've seen and admired them in zoos, and once one of them passed me in the night, rousing all the town's dogs and cats in Fernie, BC. Cougars keep the bush ecology in balance, eliminating older or crippled deer. Inquisitive animals, they sometimes follow people through the woods like a tame tabby, without anyone knowing they've been followed. Cougars are polygamous, with no fixed mating season. Males run, play, and mate with one female for several days, then hunt alone and look for another female later in their wild roaming among the mountains of northern Vancouver Island. It's a free life, a hedonistic and carefree existence that very few humans have been able to live, without the guilt and culture-pressure of being "useful to society."

Haig-Brown hasn't killed them for years, won't kill any other animal, either. There comes a time in some men's lives when killing anything is distasteful and ugly, when you take pleasure in life rather than death. As novelist and nature-writer (specializing in fishing), judge and magistrate at Campbell River, and perhaps a kind of wilderness father-figure now at age sixty-seven, that non-killing time has arrived. A medium-sized, brown-faced, balding man, he's quiet with the quietness of natural things that aren't noisy for the sake of making noise—as one must be to hear woodsmoke messages, the whisper of trees, water, and sky. He's so respected by other people that I felt incredulous when talking to them, and said to Haig-Brown himself when I met him, "You ought to have a halo, an angel's halo quivering over your head."

The catalogue of Haig-Brown's achievements runs on like a roll-call of honours. He's written some twenty-five books, all but one still in print, and considers himself a writer above all else, although he hasn't written a book in ten years because of his duties as judge in Campbell River. He feels a little guilty about that, because "a writer's business is to write. It is a defeat not to be writing." (One of the low spots in his life was when half a dozen publishers turned down a synopsis and several chapters of his fourth book, refusing to give him the $500-advance he needed desperately at the time.)

He is a literary fisherman with wide knowledge of both fish and fishing. But more important, Haig-Brown has a deep emotional involvement in all the things he writes about. He has lived and is still living a life nearly fused with nature. He's a member of the International Pacific Salmon Commission, which involves being a kind of ecology detective: "Our first objective, preservation of Pacific salmon." Among other things, " . . . we count fish—out at sea, in the catch landings (commercial fishing), on the way through the straits (Juan de Fuca and others), off the mouth of the rivers (Fraser, Adams, and Columbia), on their way up the river, on the spawning grounds—and all the way back again as the young migrate outwards. At the Adams River we stand on the bank and gloat, behaving politely to our 100,000 guests."

As a youngster in England Haig-Brown was fascinated by and in love with nature. His grandfather gave him an early affection for the woods and for the wide variety of English trees. The old man in his mid-seventies knew when particular forest stands were planted, who planted them, and why. Haig-Brown and his brothers were required to go along on extended trips through the forest, while their autocratic ancestor imparted the lore of natural things. The kids were expected to listen, respectfully attentive. Haig-Brown remembers that he learned without knowing that he did at the time.

When he was eighteen years old, Haig-Brown wanted to join the Colonial Civil Service, but was too young. Impatient to be older, he came to the United States, Washington State, in 1926, and worked at logging camps near Mount Vernon. He worked as scaler and rigger (a rigger is the guy who climbs trees and clips off their tops)—among all the other jobs like choker and chaser and faller, levermen and whistlepunks. (Logging jargon clogs into unintelligible lumps in your ears, except for the whistlepunk—who is a boy "who relays the hooktender's shouted signals by electric whistle to the donkey." Now do you know?)

Haig-Brown must have been some physically exuberant, gung-ho, cockadoodle-do kid in those days! A rather small middleweight boxer, he fought semi-pro in smokers at Sedro Woolley: you got twenty-five dollars if you won and nothing but a beating if you lost. In those days he could walk all day and climb mountains all night. He fished and hunted the lakes and forests of Washington State—and chased girls. He wrote articles for sporting magazines in England and the United States. And since he had entered the land of the free as a student and wanted to get back in legally, he went to Vancouver Island to work before returning to the States. And thought about writing his first novel. And returned to England.

Living in a rented room in London, England in 1931, he

did write that first novel. It was/is *Silver*, the story of an Atlantic salmon. He also worked in London film studios as a "wilderness expert" and "chased girls from hell to breakfast." The book was written in long-hand in ruled scribblers. And here enters the villain (or hero) that changed his life: name of *Oplopanax horridus*, the botanical term for "devil's club," a BC thorny plant cursed by early travellers and explorers in that province. While writing *Silver*, the spines of *Oplopanax horridus* festered in his arms and shoulders, popping out on the table in front of him. The discomfort in Haig-Brown's body made him homesick for Canada. He went back home to British Columbia.

In Vancouver Haig-Brown was locked up briefly at the old immigration building on Burrard Street until he could convince authorities that he wasn't a twenty-three-year-old tenderfoot Englishman who couldn't find his way in the woods from one tree to the next pub. After release, he guided tourists in the Nimpkish River area on Vancouver Island, where he had worked previously. He built his own lodge there, too, and had a registered trapline. In 1932 more logging, beachcombing, commercial fishing, bounty hunting for cougars, sport fishing, and above all writing. He was working on his next book at that time, *Pool and Rapid*.

Once he and his friends, Ed and Buster Lansdowne, heard of a freighter holed by rocks and sunk in forty feet of water off the coast of northern Vancouver Island. The three friends thought it a good chance to make some money. They bought salvage rights to the *Chackawana* from an insurance company, and devised a plan to raise the sunken ship. It was more than fifty feet long, a huge deadweight, puzzling in its salvage problems. The method finally used was pretty simple: Haig-Brown and the Lansdownes cut four huge cedar trees, hitched a steel cable under the bow of the sunken ship, and secured the other end to the logs. They repeated this procedure at the *Chackawana*'s stern—all at low tide. When moon-magic raised the tidal water and cedar logs, it also lifted the sunken freighter, whereupon the logs were shoved and towed shorewards until the *Chackawana* came to rest in shallower water.

At low tide the process was repeated, then repeated again, until finally the wrecked hulk was salvageable—a triumph of ingenuity for the three friends. Also a hard job in winter weather with high winds and the logs ice-coated, ice that sometimes caused the cables to slip and patience to explode in cusswords. Haig-Brown lived those three or four winter weeks so intensely that he remembers them well long afterwards.

Once, on the fishing boat *Kathleen* with Buster Lansdowne, they ran it into breakers in bad weather. Haig-Brown went overboard at the stern to help push the boat off, levering with the tow-post. The *Kathleen* came free suddenly and unexpectedly, leaving him hanging precariously onto the stern tow-post. Buster didn't know he was there; he assumed that Haig-Brown had enough sense to stay on the beach, safe from churning propellor blades. It was only because Buster then took the very sound precaution of walking to the stern to see if he could holler to Haig-Brown on the beach that he found him and pulled him aboard. Otherwise Roderick Haig-Brown would have been in some small danger of never writing those two dozen books.

The roving woods life began to fade away in 1934. Haig-Brown married Ann Elmore of Seattle; they bought a small farm near Campbell River and settled in to raise a family. Eventually there were four children. In 1941, at age thirty, Haig-Brown became a magistrate: "I was the only guy with time and education for the job." Hearing his first case, which involved possession of an unregistered revolver—and hearing it on the day he was sworn in—for fifteen minutes his body seized up with something like terror. "My hands shook, my eyes blurred, and my mind struggled with the spoken words as though they were a flood that would drown me."

Normally he gives the impression of a brown, quiet man, in such complete charge of himself and his own reactions that nothing flusters him; his coolness would chill beer. So it pleases me that Haig-Brown was so absolutely human on this legal occasion, and felt responsibility so strongly that he went rigid.

I kept trying to get inside this cocky kid in the woods, wearing logger's raintest with waxed knees and shoulders, chasing cougars; a small man fighting in smoky arenas and dramatically knocking out huge loggers and professional boxers. The guy who could walk all day in the bush and climb mountains all night, could haul out a 200-pound deer on his back ("I cheated and dragged it a little sometimes"), and could learn complicated things so quickly that he made the experts blush with shame. It relieves me to hear Haig-Brown say: "I get acrophobia quite easily and have to crawl in the mountains where others walked; it made me sweat to learn to climb and rig a tree and I was never easy with it."

The magistrate and judge deserves some credit for his very human wisdom: "For the most part, crime is a sad little thing, shoddy, explainable, less than vicious, almost never villainous. And the people who come into court are hard up or lazy, worried, frightened, foolish, sex-starved, or hasty, but almost never wicked." I have been all those things myself, and if I ever meet again such a heavenly judge may hope for forgiveness or at least clemency.

There is a passage in his book *Measure of the Year*, describing a 200-foot Douglas fir tree in a field near Haig-Brown's house. It is rotting to death, and has been dying for many years. "I have watched a hundred, perhaps a thousand, eagles perch in its topmost branches. I have seen it plastered with snow from ground to top . . . and watched flickers and pileated woodpeckers search its crevices for grubs." The tree is perhaps five hundred years old. It was a seedling before Shakespeare and the Wars of the Roses, before the American Revolution. It was probably born around the time Jacques Cartier slipped up the St. Lawrence River on his voyage from St. Malo to the New World. Haig-Brown speculates in his book that the tree will probably be dying still, long after his own death. But shortly after that lyrical and elegaic passage for the tree and for himself was written, the big Douglas fir blew down in a storm. "It was most embarrassing," he says, without any appearance of embarrassment.

During the early part of World War II Haig-Brown was

turned down for service because of varicose veins. A woods runner and cougar bounty hunter with varicose veins? It doesn't seem right. But he got into the army anyway (Good man!), became a captain, then a major, and as personnel officer was loaned to the RCMP. If peace hadn't come along, I'm sure he would have eventually become commanding general of all the Allied Forces in Europe. He's that sort of person, he makes me think that about him just listening and watching him while he knows I'm doing it. The gung-ho kid still lives in that middle-aged body, the cougar hunter roves in his brain, the books slide out regularly in longhand, the brown face impassive, unbetraying any pride. And myself watching—am stirred with a trace of envy. Because, despite being very human, Haig-Brown also seems just slightly Olympian. As well, there is a maverick quality about Haig-Brown, a refusal to be pigeon-holed into anything, despite all the ruts and crevices and quiet desperation we humans generally fall into.

Once, having a drink with J.H. Bloedel, the west-coast lumbering tycoon—a man who collected all sorts of valuables—Bloedel said, "I hear you're the worst trouble-maker on Vancouver Island." Which remark came as the re-sult of Haig-Brown's outright hostility to logging companies because of their ravaging the land to a naked membrane by razoring off the tall trees for timber and toothpicks.

The awkward moment passed. Bloedel showed Haig-Brown his valuable collection of what-nots and what-ises ("They're all collectors," Rod said to me later, referring to all tycoons). Then Bloedel asked him to do some writing on be-half of his lumber company.

"I don't want to be collected," the writer told the tycoon. I like that.

Haig-Brown's study-cum-library and work room is often just a place in which he can talk with friends. Today his thirty-year-old son, Alan, is there, and Alan's Indian wife. Both now live in the Chilcotin country of north-central British Columbia. Alan's father is discussed in Haig-Brown's very presence, dad remaining discreetly silent. Alan, who has worked at commercial fishing all up and down this coast of multiple bays and inlets, said: "About half the fishermen I've met had been up in court before father. They told me it wasn't the sentences he passed that bothered them so much. It was the lectures he gave them afterwards."

"Did he lecture you, too, the same way when you were a kid?" I asked Alan.

"Well, yes, so he did," Alan said.

Haig-Brown himself, depleted scotch in hand, sits like a brown buddha through this passage-at-arms, halo not even slightly askew.

The discussion turns to salmon, in all their several varieties, which have been an interest and passion for Rod Haig-Brown most of his life. His books on angling and fly-fishing are classics of the genre; some are collector's items that fetch high prices in antiquarian bookstores. Arnold Gingrich says about these books: "His writings are read, as Walton's are, as much in spite of as because of being about fishing." Which is to say that the man lives inside his writing, and outside.

In talking with Haig-Brown his opinions come across as positive – sort of radically conservative, in the sense of conserving what we have in this country. He believes that American encroachment in Canada will sort itself out: "Most countries tighten their laws about that sort of thing, as we are doing now. Eventually, if necessary, they take over foreign industry. We've been timid here in Canada, afraid of frightening away capital. The result is that we haven't made enough money from our own resources. I think that Premier Dave Barrett has the right idea about this. Profits from British Columbia industries flow south from Canada to Seattle and San Francisco – which isn't right."

About the charge that Canadians are provincial: "Of course they are! What does the cockney know of rural England, or the countryman of London? I'm not at all sure that provincialism is such an evil thing at that. No man becomes a great patriot without first learning the closer loyalties and learning them well: loyalty to the family, to the place he calls home, to his province or state or country." Haig-Brown has no patience with the recurring questions of identity that Canadians ask themselves: "That's a question manufactured by writers and intellectuals." A larger population for Canada? "I'm afraid so. We're going to have to take some of the Earth's excess people here. The world's future lies in an eventual abandonment of sovereignty." And this means world government? "Yes, we can't go in any other way. I'm not optimistic right now, but we have to work in that direction – especially when you see problems seemingly insoluble in human terms. I mean Ulster, and the Arabs and Israelis. Peace will have to be imposed." A Canadian citizen most of his life, Haig-Brown has a feeling for the country that is undefensive and unapologetic. He becomes irritated at the inferiority some Canadians claim is Canada's international status, and believes such people really have a very poor opinion of themselves.

I have two outstanding mental images of Haig-Brown. One, the kid in London, writing his first book longhand in school scribblers, while devil's club thorns pop out of his arms and shoulders. You might call that a painful reminder of citizenship. The other image is of Haig-Brown watching the old tracker, Cougar Smith, pull out the makings for a roll-your-own, then follow the trail of a mountain lion across logging slash with specs low down on his nose. Haig-Brown the judge watches the bounty hunter, watching the logger watching the married man watching the fisherman and writer – like the picture inside a picture inside a picture on the cornflakes box.

One of those pictures shows Judge Haig-Brown rushing into the court room late. He's been out fishing, and hasn't had time to change from the hip-length black rubber waders fishermen wear to whatever a judge wears. The fisherman is superimposed on the man of jurisprudence: a local citizen of Campbell River with his world-view not to be destroyed by mountain storms. And not to be collected.

Near the end of 1976 Roderick Haig-Brown died at Campbell River. I thought he would live for years, and that I'd be talking to him many times. He was a friend, and a friend to all the creatures of river and forest.

Malcolm Lowry

An unknown writer named Malcolm Lowry, living in a beach shack on Burrard Inlet near Vancouver, published a novel called *Under the Volcano* in 1947. What happened afterwards was what every writer secretly dreams of: the critics responded like trained seals – Lowry was superior to Hemingway, compared to Joyce and Thomas Wolfe; and better still, his symbolic tale about a compulsive drunk was said to be unique. Somewhat appalled by all the hoopla, Lowry reacted with a poem:

> Success is like some horrible disaster.
> Worse than your house burning, the sounds of ruination
> As the roof tree falls following each other faster
> While you stand, the helpless witness of your damnation.

He needn't have worried. A few years later and Lowry was again a nearly unknown drunk. Ten years after the novel was published, he died under mysterious circumstances in England, almost forgotten at age forty-eight. And then came the great turnaround when his posthumous reputation increased year by year. Books and magazine articles were written about him; his unfinished manuscripts were edited and published, to the accompaniment of rapturous cries of critical ecstasy. Full circle.

Considered as a human being rather than a literary genius — the way those people in close contact had to — Lowry was a failure on almost every level: a suicidal life-long alcoholic. He tried to kill himself in Acapulco by swimming farther out to sea than he had strength to return from; was attacked by a barracuda and escaped the marine assassin by taking refuge on a nearby island. In 1946 he slashed his wrists with a razor, and spent a few days in hospital recovering. He finally made it to "easeful death" in 1957 while living in the village of Ripe, in Sussex, England. Margerie, Lowry's wife, "tried to stop him from starting on the gin." She smashed the bottle, and he hit her. Margerie fled next door, afraid to return. Next morning she found him on the floor beside the smashed gin bottle. A bottle of sleeping tablets was missing. Lowry was, of course, dead.

In early summer of 1954 the dead man sat beside me in my little Ford Prefect driving from Dollarton to Vancouver to buy booze. Myself and two friends, along with Lowry and his wife, had managed to consume all there was in the beach shack. At the night liquor store near Main and Hastings, Lowry bought six bottles of Bols gin. Then he turned to me with red face and pale blue eyes and said, "There's a church near here with beautiful windows."

There actually was a church. But a man of God dressed in black was standing guard at the door. He explained to us that a wedding was about to take place and pointed out that we were not invited guests. I think he decided on first glance that we were waterfront bums, perhaps because Lowry wore an old pair of corduroy pants and black sweater. I was dressed much the same.

I explained to the priest that my friend thought the windows of his church were very beautiful and wanted to see them again. Lowry stood by silently while I talked. I tried to convey an impression of respectability and perfect sobriety, but it was difficult. We were both frankly stoned. And I had the virtuous feeling that I'd better do all the talking myself: for if Lowry spoke just once, a bottle of Bols gin was liable to pop out of his mouth and float high-away over Vancouver's skid row before the horrified eyes of the man of God.

Malcolm Lowry, born in 1909, was the youngest of four brothers. He was the son of Arthur O. Lowry, a Liverpool cottonbroker, and Evelyn Boden. Backward and shy at home, Lowry blossomed into a seeming extrovert at Cambridge University, became a champion weightlifter, golfer, swimmer, and tennis player. He also fell romantically in love with the idea of being a writer. And he was in rebellion always against authority, embodied first in the shape of father Arthur O., who had a seven-inch chest expansion and was England's best-developed man in 1904; in rebellion against uniforms, especially police uniforms; in rebellion against his wife, who came to symbolize all his own shortcomings; in rebellion, finally, against everything, including himself.

The young Lowry was first influenced by the wild tales of Jack London, and Eugene O'Neill's early sea plays. In 1927 the eighteen-year-old apprentice writer went to sea himself, having pressured Arthur O. into allowing his son to accept such plebeian employment and thus becoming a man. Poppa even chose the ship on which his son should sail as a deckhand, the *Pyrrhus*.

If a writer can ever be said to be reticent about a segment of his life used freely in his writing, Lowry was closemouthed about that voyage on the *Pyrrhus*. It did result in a youthful novel, *Ultramarine*, in 1933: and years later the same sea waves rolled through the pages of *Under the Volcano*. His writing was often nearly a direct transcript from his own life; the young sailor who early in the voyage lost most of his illusions is the same man who referred to the sea later as that "nauseous overrated expanse."

At Cambridge, Malcolm (his first name was actually Clarence, which cognomen he tried to escape all his life) played the ukelele, read many books, attended few lectures, and established the firm foundation for his later career of alcoholic consumption on a heroic scale. A member of one Charlotte

Haldane's literary salon, he was an attractive male tidbit to her, and she pursued him hill-and-dale all over the salon.

An American poet and novelist, Conrad Aiken, then living in England, appeared on the scene in 1928. Lowry worshipped the older man's writing. Deciding that he preferred this surrogate father to his own, he prevailed on Arthur O. to allow him to join Aiken when the latter returned home to the Land of the Free—in return for a weekly stipend to Aiken of five or six guineas, of course.

In Boston the aspiring young writer and the older poet hit it off perfectly. Aiken has often said of the relationship, "We were natural father and son." But that first evening together doesn't sound like a loving *pater* and dutiful sibling. They threw a wild party, in which the finale was a wrestling match between Lowry and Aiken for possession of a porcelain toilet seat. Weightlifter Malcolm tossed his surrogate father into the stone fireplace and fractured his skull. "That," says Aiken, "was the beginning of a beautiful friendship."

So I talked. The dead man and the priest listened. A car drew up at the curb during my unpersuasive discourse, disgorging some wedding guests. The man of God hurried to greet them. While he did so, I was suddenly shocked to realize that Lowry had disappeared as my harangue continued, and had simply walked into the church. I'd been the unflattering red herring for his entrance, as now the wedding guests were for mine.

Lowry knelt on the floor inside the church, praying to some God or other, with six bottles of Bols gin in a brown paper grocery bag on the seat behind him. I thought of Coleridge's Ancient Mariner. And Lowry dressed in a strange medieval seaman's costume: hung around his neck, instead of a dead albatross, six bottles of Bols gin in a brown grocery bag. Then, with burning eyes, he began collaring the wedding guests at the curb outside, whisking one of them away from the officious priest. "Listen," he would say to the wedding guest, "once, in a Mexican town called Quauhnahuac, there was a consul. —"

After sitting at Aiken's feet, picking his brains for clues to genius, drinking and carousing with him, Lowry returned to England and Cambridge University. And more drinking,

drinking, drinking. Arthur O. gave him an allowance of seven pounds a week, but on condition that he appear personally to collect it at the company's London office. Malcolm refused to go – he was too dirty, and had no shoes, and didn't want to shave.

What kind of writer-genius, as apart from an ordinary human being, does all this signify? Self-indulgent, spoiled, drunken, prey to wild fantasies, archetype of all the self-destructive people with time-bombs ticking in their heads since time began. But one fact emerges over all others: Lowry thought that life was hell, and he was delineating the map of hell in all he lived and wrote.

If Lowry had been just an ivory-tower aesthete, concerned only with his navel (which he was, among other things), we humans could all dismiss him with the customary shrug we reserve for boring TV programs. But pain, embarrassment, horror, shame, and all those words streaming out of our guts are common to all of us; if one is in a depressed state, their sum total might actually be called "hell." Lowry contains all our hells – and did even when he was twenty-two years old.

On our second visit to the beach shack, the dead man went swimming in Burrard Inlet, his red face and barrel chest bobbing around in the cold water like pieces of coloured driftwood. Later, it seemed completely natural that my friend and I, Lowry and his wife, drank Bols gin, which sometimes replaced coffee and tea in that household.

It grew darker then. Across black water silver candles of the oil refinery lit the early evening, the same ones Lowry called, ironically, "the loveliest of oil refineries." He and my friend sang songs outside, while I sat at Lowry's typewriter and copied his poems by lamplight, feeling very literary and virtuous.

They were odd, doom-laden poems, very regular and formal, maybe even Elizabethan-sounding, death implicit in all of them. But in each poem, generally at the end, a line or two would silently go "boom": a phrase incandescent –

No Kraken shall depart till bade by name,
No peace but that must pay full toll to hell.

Then the rough-tender voices of my friends, the literary drunks, floated

through the window to join in my mind the many-tentacled Kraken:
"Away, away, away you rolling river."

In 1933 Lowry lived in Paris for a time with Julian Trevelyan, the painter. Then he accompanied Conrad Aiken and the latter's second wife to Spain, where Lowry drank heavily, grew fat, and became known as *el borracho ingles,* known also to the Spanish Civil Guard. While there he met an attractive American girl, Jan Gabrial. Lowry sobered immediately, and fell in love.

Leaving Spain, the Aikens and Lowry sailed for England, and Malcolm shared a cabin with "three Somerset Maughan colonels who were dying of the hiccups." The floating circus then played a few months of one-night stands in Mexico. By this time Lowry had caught up with the luscious Jan Gabrial, and married her. The relationship made progress: he drunk in Cuernavaca; she living somewhere else. Aiken observed all this with pity and horrified love; both of them writing, writing, writing. . . .

"He's drinking the alarm clock," cried Jan at Cuernavaca after the Aikens were gone. "I just don't care about him, but I can't buy another alarm clock." Apparently Lowry had abducted the timepiece to pawn it and buy booze. But if Lowry was no more valuable than an alarm clock to Jan, then apparently the end of their marriage could be predicted. It was. Jan soon departed for other ports of call.

Lowry stayed on in Mexico, through more alcoholic misadventures: went to jail in Oaxaca ("where they cure syphilis with Sloans liniment / And clap with another dose"); and wandered the bone-dry hills of central Mexico with a friend. Expelled from Mexico, he ended up in Los Angeles, where Arthur O. came to the rescue of his prodigal son (Arthur O. used that very phrase to describe him). In the American film capital Lowry met Margerie, whom he loved – and hated – and married.

The dead man was cheerful, dreadfully potted and sounding very
English, but still alive. During the long evening of Bols gin and talk,
Lowry recited his poem, "Sestina in a Cantina," his thick voice bear-

ing the full weight of archaic fear and horror: how the world is a giant prison ruled by tossing mooseheads and witchdoctors in business suits. And Lowry talked about the weird sorcerers of Central America, their seeming imperviousness to the pain of red-hot coals, how sailors all seem to be part mystic and. . . .

Falling silent, he stared at nothing in front of him, as if the room were completely empty. Perhaps thinking of tossing mooseheads that ruled the world? Or the match-like spurt of distant flame on its lone steel swan's neck at the oil refinery across the inlet? Of ships that sailed forever, revisiting old ports over and over again, bells clanging out of time:

In sleep all night he grapples with a sail'
But words beyond the life of ships dream on.

That first meeting of Margerie Bonner and Lowry at the corner of Hollywood Boulevard and Western was a passionate embrace. Margerie, a former movie starlet and radio writer, was general factotum to actress Penny Singleton. Married to her drunken literary genius, she emerged as a woman of character and strength, and probably discovered more drama in her life with Lowry than existed in the entire dream city of Hollywood.

The Lowrys moved to Vancouver in 1939, and fell almost immediately into the clutches of one Maurice Carey, a retired sergeant-major from the Canadian army. Lowry's monthly allowance from Arthur O. was nonsensically signed over to Carey. In return Carey gave the Lowrys an unheated attic room for lodgings and two dollars a week for spending money. From this unhappy haven Lowry disappeared on one cold and rainy October night. Margerie found him in a Vancouver whorehouse, where he had sold his clothes to buy a bottle of gin. She threatened the madam into giving her man's clothes back to him, and they went out into the rain, he doubled over with shame and a hangover.

In 1940 the Lowrys found their shack on Burrard Inlet. It was one of some fifteen such jerry-built structures, with low rent because the land was owned by Vancouver's Harbour

Board. This was Lowry's Eden, his Walden Pond, and it supplied material and experience for *The Forest Path to the Spring*, as fine a work as he ever wrote. When the shack burned down, the Lowrys scrounged enough money to build another. Here also much of the final draft of *Under the Volcano* was transferred to paper from Lowry's head. Often he would hand his wife a page he had just written and say, "Margie, kindly tell me what the hell I'm talking about here." Which is to say that Margerie herself deserved much credit for the novel that some say is the greatest written in the twentieth century.

The fourteen years at Dollarton (until 1954) were interspersed with trips to other parts of the world, including Mexico, from which Lowry was again expelled for non-payment of a small fine that he had been assessed years before. Also interspersed with frequent gargantuan benders, of which he once said that "he was pitting, like Paracelsus, the effects of alcohol against the effects of increased physical exercise . . . to drink through and out the other side of a nervous breakdown, or worse." A strange reason for keeping the distilleries working at full capacity. But much of Lowry's lifetime was spent either drinking or taking treatment for drinking, the latter sometimes in hospitals or similar institutions. And the pure horror he experienced in not being cured seems far worse than the horror of drinking itself.

Many people would consider Malcolm Lowry a failure, but if so, surely he was an immortal failure. He had many qualities of those other historic drunks, Brendan Behan and Dylan Thomas: people loved him, for instance. They arranged things for him, smoothed his way if they could, and came when he called to them in desperation. And much of his life was desperation! In some ways Lowry was not a weak man: witness the fierce and continual devotion to writing. Which itself is a reflection of himself and his conviction that living life is experiencing a nether hell.

To be alive is to have the skin prickle, the genitals cringe at what happens to all of us: and what happens to all of us also happened in intensified form to Lowry. He was a feeler

–and experiencer–of the lower depths. And sometimes out of this evil human world suddenly appeared human-created good.

The reasons why Lowry wrote–both loving and hating writing–might be summed up in that couplet about the Kraken who must not be named, and the peace that has to be paid for by a preceding hell. Hell must be mapped and named, the beasts of our minds exorcised with words of knowledge. Therefore Malcolm Lowry wrote about his own personal predicament, which is also the human predicament –and no other species can make that statement.

For several months after the Lowrys went to Europe in 1954, I was involved with introducing a union into the mattress factory on Clarke Drive, where I worked. Then I returned to the beach shack near Dollarton with my friend and a beautiful girl. We brought along a bottle of wine to drink, pouring the heel of it into the sea at the end of Lowry's dock. A selfconscious gesture, a libation to Bacchus and Lowry, an act whose meaninglessness somehow stands out in my mind.

Drinking coffee with Irving Layton at Murray's Restaurant in Montreal in 1957, Layton told me that Lowry was dead in England. I felt suddenly desolate.

But Lowry surfaced again in 1962, when I read his posthumous book of stories, Hear Us O Lord from Heaven Thy Dwelling Place, *with its recurring song of a ship's engines. And freighters are still moving outward from Burrard Inlet toward the Lions Gate through the fog, past the razed shack at the sea's edge, throb of engines whispering among the trees near an overgrown path through the forest:*

Frère Jacques
Frère Jacques
Dormez-vous?
Dormez-vous?

Imagine a Town

Imagine a town that sits on the edge of a great blue inland sea, where polar bears roam day and night across the garbage dump (as many as eighteen have been sighted at one time, and part of the local taxes is used for cherry bombs that sound like the Amchitka explosion to drive the great beasts farther north); where a Chipewyan Indian Village, an Eskimo settlement, straggling métis houses, and the white man's city stand close together but never quite mix; where white whales lollop and roll near the river mouth, in sunlight so brilliant that it makes shadows seem more real than buildings.

The town is Churchill, Manitoba, on Hudson Bay, with a population of 10,000 and a deep-sea port that shipped 25,-000,000 bushels of wheat across the Atlantic in 1970. I arrived there near midnight, having taken the night plane from Winnipeg to Churchill. Next morning I drove around the town with Ernie Senior, manager of the port of Churchill, as well as publisher of the local newspaper. Ernie is short, middle-aged, balding, and a bubbly enthusiast for the good things about this small Arctic city. The arctic–or, in this case, the sub-arctic–seems to abound with people like that, who love the north and want to publicize it. Three or four years ago he was an adviser to Warner Troyer when the latter made a CBC documentary about Indian social conditions in Churchill–which were not very good at the time, although they have become slightly, infinitesimally better now.

Ernie talks non-stop about Churchill: a new recreation centre for the Chipewyans, whale hunting for tourists (eighty bucks a day and a two-whale limit for each big-game hunter), the sheer exhilaration of breathing clean wine-like unpolluted air, and Ernie's own pet project of a northern university here, using the near-billion-dollars-worth of government buildings now gradually being phased out at Fort Churchill.

Years ago Ernie Senior was an Anglican missionary paid one hundred dollars a month, sometimes spending a large part of that salary feeding starving Indians and Eskimos. After leaving the priesthood he did a little of everything before coming to his present job. I had lunch that day with Ernie and his wife, a brisk, cordial woman who dispensed hospitality as if strangers like myself were old friends and never an inconvenience.

In the afternoon Ernie and I did the grand tour of Churchill again: visiting huge grain elevators on the edge of Henry Hudson's sea; cruising slowly through the garbage dump, where one cantankerous-looking female polar bear lifted her swaying head wickedly, then went back to eating delicious garbage; touring the Indian recreation building, whose functions were explained to me briefly by a Chipewyan youth with a stoned expression; and talking to a man building his own cottage near a shallow inland lake. "Just to get away from the crowds," he said. Crowds? I think that the arctic population works out to one-and-a-quarter bodies per square mile, give or take an arm or a leg.

Near the Churchill River mouth I stared across at the

stone ruins of Fort Prince of Wales, on a narrow promontory jutting into the sea, with cannon peering across the empty horizon. The stone fort is 300 feet square and the walls forty feet thick. During the war between Britain and France in 1782, La Perouse, the French admiral, captured it without firing a shot. At that time there were only thirty-nine men defending a fort meant to be staffed by 400. The immense empty stoneworks lie there in sunlight like a stranded grey whale, forever useless except as a magnet for tourist dollars.

Rattling around with Ernie over the bumpy roads of Churchill, I thought of Frobisher Bay on Baffin Island, where I had spent an Arctic summer six years before. It was barren, desolate, and all those other adjectives writers use about the north. But maybe there's something wrong with me, for I don't feel those things, as some others do. Sure, I'll be out of here damn quick after today, but the things I see are people, most of all—and the huge elemental map of land and sky and sea, on which everything is stripped to essentials. People are only and first of all people, and not executives and cost accountants; here they retain their humanity. Land is stripped to earth or to the bare stone of the Canadian Shield, and the sky and sea explode with their own blue being.

Not everyone feels this way about the north. And maybe all of us citizens of the southern north and the northern north *are* money-grubbers on the lookout for the big buck. Money is certainly necessary to life; we're realists and pragmatists in the sense that we live day to day and go where the money is to do it; but beyond that there has to be something; for some a god, for others a woman, and perhaps friends. Well, I don't despise those other things, but I think that the sheer concepts of land and country—contained by reality and echoed in the mind—these also are indispensable to myself.

I suppose that's one of the reasons I liked Ernie Senior, because of similar feelings to mine that I sensed in him. He's a talkative little man, a verbose publicist for the north, but I'm sure with a great emotional blaze in himself for things around him. The sky overhead, the rocky pancake land with its savage, arrogant, man-killing weather, the map in himself of summer and winter, the Anglican priest that he was and the Churchill port manager that he is now: and the human being that includes them all.

I was thinking of all this when Ernie drove me to the train, and as I travelled all night and the next day southward to meet my wife at The Pas. And of Churchill with its exhilaration and its squalor, parked beside Henry Hudson's sea; with the go-getting merchants and soon on-coming wheeler-dealers and fast bucks; and with Indians sitting out their exile from the just society. And of the strangeness of riding a train south from the barren ground and being myself. Imagine Churchill.

Dryland Country

It's like coming out of a dark room – to leave the hills and leafless forests of an Ontario countryside on a dull April day, to find yourself under the white blaze of a Saskatchewan sky. Transport by Air Canada to the prairies in three swift hours requires some mental adjustments on arrival; my body has already made them, but the mind is still getting used to this new landscape. Then driving west from Regina along the Trans-Canada over some of the best wheatland in the world, flat as a tabletop, turning south on highway 21 at Maple Creek and surrounded by low treeless olive-coloured hills, I'm feeling more at home. It's still Canada. Stopping to stretch my legs, I'm the one vertical thing in a country where all else is horizontal. I rather like the feeling; it gives some unique importance to myself. I think many of the people here must feel the same way.

The reason for my trip is to visit the site of a proposed Grasslands Park in the southwest corner of Saskatchewan. The joint Federal-Provincial park will occupy some 350 square miles in two separate parcels of land connected by a park road, an East Block and a West Block near the towns of Val Marie, Killdeer and Mankota. It will, that is, when and if the park proposals are fully implemented. Its purpose is to ensure that "a remnant of the prairies grasslands would be set aside and interpreted for this and future generations." Prairie dog towns along the Frenchman River valley are the only ones in Canada where this animal can be observed in its natural habitat.

But there's a fly in the ointment—for Parks Canada and the provincial authorities at Regina. The proposed parkland is already occupied by more than prairie dogs, golden eagles, hawks, coyotes and rattlesnakes. People live there too. Thirty-nine families of ranchers are directly dependent on this land, either living there on land partly leased, or in nearby areas. Their holdings include some 6,000 head of cattle; most of their sons and daughters were born and raised on this sunlit tableland. The ranchers object to being displaced in favour of prairie dogs.

I'm approaching the disputed rangeland through the back door, via the Cypress Hills. These Hills have what I think is the most interesting and colourful history in Canada, which is a flat statement of fact. They are situated on the Saskatchewan border, directly adjoining the US border, rising a little more than 4,800 feet above sea level, hence more than a thousand feet above the surrounding rangeland. Seventy million years ago a shallow body of water, called the Bearpaw Sea by geologists, covered the central continent from the Gulf of Mexico to the Arctic Ocean, including all of the area I'm now visiting. Dinosaurs ramped at the edge of this Bearpaw Sea; exotic vegetation flourished there before and after the Rocky Mountains were born. The thirty-five foot king tyrannosaurus, with teeth like small swords, chased the gentle vegetarian reptiles along those shores. Later in geologic time, there were sabre-toothed cats, camels and titanotheres. All this long before the embattled ranchers and their dispute with Parks Canada.

During the last Ice Age, 20,000 years ago, glaciers blanketed these northern plains. But the Hills (which are actually a dissected flat-topped plateau) were never entirely covered by ice. It flowed around and crossed between them at an opening called "The Gap." An island of eighty or ninety square miles lifted above the frozen desert, and diverted the slow stampede of ice on either side.

Animals fled to this high plateau as ice groaned and splintered along the flanks of the Hills, warning that the Earth-Shaker was upon them. It was a refuge, a biological island, preserving Rocky Mountain plants and animals far into the plains, and southern species far into the north. In Anno Domini 1977, it's a park.

I stop at the park buildings, deserted except for one lonesome secretary, to eat sandwiches and drink a beer. Not far from where I'm having lunch, eighty Assiniboins under Chief Little Soldier were massacred by American wolvers and whiskey traders in 1873, at Moses Solomon's trading post. All around me spruce, pine and aspen stir peacefully in the April wind, as if nothing had ever happened here. But as a result of the massacre came the Royal North West Mounted Police, the Mounties. And with their arrival things did stop happening, at least to the extent that full-scale wars between Blackfoot and other tribes ended; the whiskey traders went out of business, or back south, or became mere bootleggers. When Sitting Bull fled to Wood Mountain, north of the border Medicine Line, after trouncing Custer at Little Big Horn, the Mounties told him to behave himself. And rather amazingly, he did.

Nobody quite knows how the Mounties were able to accomplish such sweetness and light in such a notably lawless country. But they did. And the us Army, those blue-shirted "Long Knives" watching their fugitive Indians escape the American way of death north of the Medicine Line, may also have wondered a little how the trick was done.

Fifteen miles south of the Cypress Hills with their relatively abundant rainfall, I turn east into arid semi-desert. Trees become a rarity; gophers popping up on either side of the road look thirsty. Prairie towns skim past, Robsart, Eastend, Shaunavon, and finally Val Marie. The landscape is low rolling olive-coloured hills, part of the hundred miles of rangeland country between the Cypress Hills and Wood Mountain. It's also part of Palliser's Triangle (he was a British explorer in this neck of the prairie in 1857, who said the country was entirely worthless).

Val Marie looks like most small prairie towns: population about 250, down from 500; a little more shabby than is usual; grain elevators are vertical coloured blocks against the sky; an early spring sun searing everyone off the street except a dog on the hotel porch, panting. In the pub I ask directions how to find the dissident ranchers. It turns out a few are in favour of the park, most notably Francis Walker.

Outside Val Marie I join Wally Carlier, his wife, and Merv Timmon, a rancher-farmer, drinking coffee in the Carlier kitchen. Mrs. Wally is the town clerk, and won't say much about the park because of her official position. Merv Timmon, sandy-haired and about forty-five, is more outgoing. He says the park is "the craziest thing I ever heard of." Well, that's more like it: a strong positive opinion. Timmon goes on, "Ranchers don't interfere with the natural state of the land, so why spend millions preserving it the way it already is?"

When and if the proposed park is implemented, it will directly adjoin the American border. And there's an International Agreement with the Americans that they will receive half the natural run-off from the creeks that drain south into the US. However, at the present time they receive much more than half of these downstream water benefits in this near-desert country. Reason: there are no dams north of the border. If the park is implemented (and a report of the Public Hearings Board indicates it will be), then such building projects as dams will not be permitted. The Frenchman River and several smaller creeks drain this area in southern Saskatchewan of precious water, and there's been no appreciable rain since August, 1976. The final yes or no decision about the park will be made June 30, 1977.

That's about the extent of my park knowledge until I talk

to Norm Kornfeld and his wife Doris on their ranch about eight miles south of Val Marie. Norm is forty-two, heavy-set, side-burned and slightly balding. Doris is thirty-eight, not very big and quite a pretty woman. The Kornfelds have thirteen sections of crown land under government lease (a section is 640 acres), and run 225 head of cattle. Norm and his family came here in 1964 from Verwood farther north, and operated the ranch in partnership with his dad, who is now retired. Son Glen, seventeen, and daughter Gail, six-teen, both grew up on the ranch. They say they'd "feel a kind of emptiness if we lose the land."

"People ask why we need so much land," Norm Kornfeld says. "Well, they don't realize that a section of land can only feed about two dozen cows in this dry country." I drink some more coffee and read the brief Norm presented at the park hearing in Val Marie: "I have spent the past twelve years, the most productive years of my life, transforming this ranch to its present modern state of corrals, barns, water and sewage facilities and a new home. Now I have less than ten minutes to present a brief about why I wish to re-main in this part of the country and fulfil my childhood dream of being a successful rancher."

I can see what he means, and those dozen years out of his life are all around us. No, it doesn't seem entirely fair to me either.

The three of us, Norm, Doris and myself, board his four-wheel-drive truck to visit the prairie dog colony near the Frenchman River bottomlands. (And the only way you can get around in this country, aside from horses is by four driving wheels.)

We jolt over the winding road that's more track than road, and more trail than track, me braced against the bumps, stopping at a high butte where you can see the green-bordered Frenchman River snaking across the prairie. It's all the green there is. On the bottomlands a nation of black-tailed prairie dogs has pimpled the ground with earth beside their holes. Their heads pop up; they make a noise like some weird bird, going "cheep-cheep." I guess it means

"Danger! Two-legged critters on the prowl. Watch yourself!"

Norm draws a map to give me directions for Bruce Dixon's ranch, twenty-five miles away. And says at the door, "We won't leave this ranch!"

Bruce Dixon is forty, his wife Stella, thirty-eight. We drink coffee in the Dixon kitchen. He says, "They protect prairie dogs, why not protect people?" It's a question with some resentment, and I can't answer him. They've been on the land since 1955, the year a very young Bruce and his dad built their first log house. Since then the son has gradually taken over ranch operations from his father. Bruce and Stella have two children, the usual heavy investment in buildings and machinery, without much return since beef prices have been low for some time. Like the Kornfelds, they're on call every three hours, to assist or provide aid and comfort to cows giving birth at this season of the year.

The Dixons lease and own forty-two sections of rangeland, a much larger outfit than Norm Kornfeld's place. "What happens to you when beef prices are so low?" I want to know. "You ever feel like giving up and going to work in a factory?"

Bruce Dixon smiles. "We just tighten our belts. And wait." The smile is maybe a little forced, but he's right; all anyone can do is wait until things get better. "And we won't move," he says, "no matter what."

Every ranch house I visit gives me a map showing me how to get to the next; and I've drunk so much coffee I hate the stuff. I've seen no people on this dirt track that seems to lead nowhere. Then a string of about twenty horses sweeps around a curve, startled by the car, manes tossing and colours brilliant in the sun: chestnuts, greys, black and whites, half-wild and wholly graceful. A youngster on a black horse follows them, and I think he can't be more than eighteen. The hat sweeps off in greeting, and they're gone around another bend in the road, a small cloud of dust rising and disappearing.

Occasionally there's a deserted house to arouse my curiosity. I stop at one of them, jump over a small creek, my feet nervous from possible rattlesnakes. The house is stone with mortar decayed, the shingled roof fallen in, its interior a mass of broken chairs, tangled bedsprings and household wreckage. It must be years since anyone has lived there. When I stick my head inside a broken windowframe, a dozen birds nearly decapitate me in their frenzied escape outward.

Reconnoitering for a non-muddy place to cross the creek again, wind tugs at my clothes insistently. It is a prairie constant, that wind. Overhead clouds sail eastward before it like ships; here on the ground everything moves in brief unison, whether plant or animal; it handles grass and the most delicate small flowers, twitching the fur of rabbits and prairie dogs, a continual part of their lives. In winter it rides the Chinook across mountains, moving snow with invisible hands, and some snow still remains in early spring. And there are voices contained by the wind, non-human voices, as if it were the thing Shanley referred to in his verse:

Sancta Maria, speed us!
The sun is falling low;
Before us lies the valley
Of the Walker of the Snow.

Don Gillespie is balding and big, I'd guess about 210 pounds, and very quiet. Maybe that's because his wife, Norah, is vivacious and not given to long silences. They are both forty-eight. Four generations of the family live at the ranch. Norah's dad and his brother, Lloyd Way, came here in 1915, and built a 14' by 16' shack on the land. Norah's Uncle Lloyd is now eighty-three, becoming a little pale and fragile. "But he still works," Norah insists. Lloyd grins. "Not now."

I mention the deserted house I passed on the way here. "It was abandoned in the mid-forties," Don says. Son Darwin, fourteen, says there's the remains of a sod house not far from here. "But there's not much left of it, only the four corners." No wonder it's vanishing into the ground it came from, built only of sod and grass roots. A man named Fred Hausman died there some time in the thirties.

About the park, Norah says, "We don't intend to leave, but they might starve us out. The government could cancel our leases at any time." The Gillespies are not precisely scornful about the park, since we all agree that preserving the prairie ecology is a good thing. But living where you've lived all your life, and where you expect your bones to be part of the land eventually–that too is important. Norah says that on their forty-plus sections of rangeland, "We want to raise the best bunch of cattle that ever roamed the prairies." Then she adds thoughtfully, "We grow live things." She means, I guess, that ranching is different from turning out plastic do-dads or manufacturing steel automobiles in concrete factories; in fact, it's different from anything but ranching. Perhaps because all of us are live things.

Leaving the Gillespie place, I take a wrong turn. It's several miles before I notice I'm somewhat lost, and that the dirt track over the prairie isn't taking me anywhere. Everything looks like everything else; no landmarks whatever. Of course it's no big deal, but I can't turn around in my rented car because of the shallow ditches and some ugly-looking rocks. Thirty feet from the road a brown and white cow is sleeping. How nice, how peaceful and rural! But when I pass by a little farther there's daylight shining through the cow's body from end to end; it's entirely hollow. Nothing there but hide and bones and hooves, a skin tent. It does give you a little chill at such times. Olive-coloured rangeland all around, with late patches of snow scattered here and there, nothing alive but prairie dogs and rattlesnakes–and myself for a while longer.

The Paris Hotel at Mankota is not exactly reminiscent of the City of Light, but it's comfortable. The town itself has about 400 people, with no livery stable despite it being cowboy country. Those are off the movie set in Hollywood. I have something to eat and a few beer, talk to the barkeep, play some pool and go to bed.

Sometime in the night I find myself standing beside an

encampment of Red River carts, the same kind used to help settle the nineteenth century prairies. I'm slightly aware that it's a dream, because I'm still tired in the dream after several days driving and talking in Saskatchewan. But a dream is something you can't swear isn't real when you're right inside it. The carts are stopped along a river valley, but too large a river to be the Frenchman. I walk around them, pleased they're not moving, because when they do move there's a noise like a thousand devils filing saws to cut off the legs of shrieking sinners in hell. Made entirely of wood, there's no grease in the axles, because dust would seize them up. And I seem to wonder: do these carts belong to métis on a buffalo hunt in the last century? Or the Overlanders of 1862 on their way across the plains, bound for the Cariboo gold fields?

There's moonlight, pale stuff tinging the encampment with dusty silver. No horses. Nothing alive that I can see. But they must have left a guard somewhere. No hunting party would sleep without one. And I'm right. He's down by the river, a dark hawk-nosed man, probably métis, sound asleep. His long-barrelled rifle is held in his right hand, a Sharps, I think; the kind "that shoots today and kills tomorrow." They were a favourite of buffalo hunters. The rifle's wooden stock is beaded with condensed mist, and as I watch a small drop of water trickles irregularly down the polished wood, disappearing in grass.

A dream. Next I'll be dreaming of the Bearpaw Sea, with dinosaurs in full colour? Anyway, I make a note of it when I wake up in the morning.

The barkeep is a genial sort of guy, and invites me to visit a rattlesnake pit with him. These are depressed places in the prairie, into which gophers or burrowing owls have driven their own burrows. And since reptiles can't dig holes, they simply take over from creatures who can. But it's too early in the spring for snakes to be above ground; the spade-shaped heads and buggy-whip bodies are coiled sluggishly under the earth in reptilian dreams.

In May, 1976, one hundred and eight briefs were submitted to a Public Hearings Board, which was "appointed to advise the Government of Saskatchewan on the degree of public support for the proposed Grasslands National Park." These hearings were held at Regina, Saskatoon, Killdeer, Mankota and Val Marie. Obviously, the peope who submitted briefs in Saskatoon and Regina were not generally involved directly with the area concerned (as some ranchers I talked to pointed out). Briefs from urban areas were almost entirely in favour of the park; ranching areas were largely against it.

And some insights into the situation might be derived from the briefs themselves. I found it interesting that the learned societies and ecology people presented papers in rather pedantic language, sometimes crowded with statistics which they felt proved their point in favouring the park.

Several of the ranchers' briefs were in longhand, and their grammar wasn't always perfect. They tended to be a little emotional at times, which is easy to understand. They were outnumbered by professors and civil servants; a few sound slightly paranoic, as if they've already lost the struggle for *their* land. And I think they have. I think the government has already decided, despite the deadline for decision on the park being June 30, 1977.

The rancher-wives are often more articulate than their men. Mrs. Marjorie Linthicum, from a ranch near Kildeer, says: "I wouldn't like to see the ranches destroyed and their remains become a monument of the past, as are dinosaur bones, teepee rings of the Indians, and the many rows of rock piles of the early settlers which are all so familiar in some of the area I speak of. I have spent many days riding over this land. I know what it's like to ride all day and never encounter another soul; to have a faithful horse bring me sixteen miles home through a blinding storm; to drive cattle home in the fall and have them strung out for two or three miles heading for their winter pastures; to sit on a knoll and watch cattle graze on an alkali flat, or two mighty bulls battle over a harem of cows; to repair fence all day and pick wood ticks off all evening; to see bands of wild horses trailed out to packing plants because of modernization; to sit on a high butte and look south over the prairie for miles; to drive cows and calves to summer pasture and then sit on a hillside and watch till they mother-up; to dream as a young girl of riding south to the badlands and driving cattle with my dad and then having my dreams come true; to trail carloads of grass-fed beef thirty miles to the railway in thirty-five degree-below weather; to see buffalo horns on the prairie and wonder if it died from a winter storm or an Indian arrow; to have your horse get loose and leave you fifteen miles from home. Perhaps I am selfish, but I would like my family and their heirs to be able to enjoy this part of my heritage as much as I have. I feel I am as much part of this land as are the coyotes and gophers."

And that says it all.

Driving east to Regina the wind is blowing, a heavy gusting wind that scoops topsoil off the farmland, and turns the ploughed fields pale and ghostly. It makes you think of the bad dustbowl days in the dry thirties, especially when the white stuff you're driving through is the actual soil of somebody's farmland. It makes all our hopes for the future seem no more substantial than white mist, a floury dust that coats the car's interior plastic but can't be baked into bread. Only the gold stubble-land of last year's crop resists the scouring wind.

It's a strange and tragic feeling to be driving through somebody's dreams at about 65 miles per hour. It makes me think of the Biblical Seven Lean Years in Egypt here on the prairies, with all the Pharaoh's storage houses and our own red grain elevators filled – filled with nothing but dust.

But that feeling is still only a dark mood, which may yet turn to silver in the falling rain. Southwest of here, and all across the untracked ranges, cows are dropping their young in an orgy of birth. Thousands of calves are staggering to their feet and searching blindly for their mother's milk. The rancher midwives attend them: sympathetic, but cussing sometimes from lack of sleep. In the Cypress Hills, spring stirs, grass awakes. Soon the sun will trigger flowers like small red jewels nearly hidden in winter's brown slag.

It takes a small leap of the imagination to realize that all of this brown land, soon turning to green and gold, was once the Bearpaw Sea seventy million years ago. Hereford and Charolais and other cattle breeds have replaced the dinosaurs. As prong horn deer have replaced camels and titanotheres. In a much later time, whites have replaced the Indians and métis. It's impossible to conceive an equal leap into the future or whether there will still be men at all in that distant time. But if there are, I hope some may be ranchers.

Streetlights on the St. Lawrence

Canada is a country where the heartland, centres of commerce and population, are almost entirely inland. The Atlantic traveller approaching the United States is suddenly confronted with the whole North American continent – it lifts right out of the sea at New York, and you're surrounded by people with scarcely any transition. But the traveller or immigrant bound for Montreal may enter the great watery jaws between Newfoundland and Cape Breton and be surrounded by five provinces of the new country without even knowing it. Distances in the Gulf of St. Lawrence are so immense that there often could be no land within sight of the marine traveller.

Nineteenth-century immigrants, particularly, must have observed with alarm and sometimes fear the rugged olive-green hills of the North Shore and the mountains of Gaspé drifting past. Some of them may have known that Jacques Cartier called this place of water and stone "the land God gave to Cain" – which seems to me a little extreme, even for an explorer from sunny France. But after voyages sometimes lasting many weeks, cooped-up on ships that must have seemed prisons, the dispossessed Scottish crofters and survivors of the Irish potato famine surely had a right to hope for something better. And to the women and their sometimes half-starved children this new world must have seemed much worse than the old. They were lost in this desolate place, thousands of miles from friends and relatives, without even control of their own bodies and destinies.

In late May, 1974, I reversed the westward track of those nineteenth-century immigrants. Boarding the 8,500 ton lake freighter *Golden Hind* at Thorold on the Welland Canal, Captain Cecil Freeman commanding, I travelled eastward through Lake Ontario and the St. Lawrence Seaway, eventually reaching Baie Comeau on the Quebec North Shore. The ship's cargo was soy beans and corn from Chicago; she carried a crew of thirty-one. At Baie Comeau I left the *Golden Hind* and flew back to Montreal, with the feeling of having added another thousand miles of previously unknown territory to the place in mind that is Canada.

Traversing the seaway was like driving a car, then coming to a whole series of maddening red lights: stop and go, stop and go. We would enter a lock, wait, water pouring out of the concrete playpen with a whoosh, and drop some fifty feet. Then zoom-zoom go the engines and we're on our way to the next traffic light. Moving slowly down the Welland Canal, the whole green country of the Niagara Peninsula is dwarfed – trees, houses, people, everything. The 620-foot-long ship is simply monstrous. And your mind has to handle it somehow. I managed that by saying to myself that lakers like the *Golden Hind* – as well as larger ships – are only boxes made of steel being pushed somewhere by wound-up rubberbands, or some other motive power invented by people. It's less grandiose that way.

The original *Golden Hind* weighed one hundred tons and was probably not more than seventy-five feet long, with a crew of around one hundred. Francis Drake circumnavigated the world with this ship in 1580, an age when many people still thought the Earth was flat and you'd fall off at the other side. Drake was an English pirate and patriot, a religious man who had prayers on shipboard twice a day, and who thought there was nothing irreligious about sacking a Spanish town in the Caribbean Sea between prayers. And yet when Francis Fletcher, his chaplain, criticized him slightly for poor seamanship, Drake padlocked Fletcher to a hatch and excommunicated him in the sight of God and man and the devil. The fair-haired freebooter, sitting cross-legged on a sea chest, ordered that a band be placed around his chaplain's arm that proclaimed the wearer "Francis Fletcher, the falsest knave that liveth." Which seems to indicate that if you don't agree with a captain while at sea you'd better keep the disagreement to yourself.

But Captain Cecil Freeman is nothing like Sir Francis Drake, he's a six-foot-tall, heavily built middle-aged Newfoundlander, and with a nice sense of humour. In the wheelhouse of the *Golden Hind*, between saying to the wheelsman, "Steer between those two buoys," he talks to me about getting a ticket for speeding from the US Coastguard.

"I was master of the *S.S. Thorold* a few years back, and they told me on the radio-telephone that I'd exceeded the fifteen-miles-per-hour speed limit."

"And you hadn't?"

"It's like talking to the cops, they hear only their own side of anything. When you argue you make it worse. But I won this argument."

"How?"

"Well, they measure your speed by the period of time it takes for the distance between the ship's bow and stern to pass a fixed point on land. It's all done mechanically and pretty hard to disagree with. But in this case they had the wrong ship."

"Huh?"

"There happened to be another, earlier *S.S. Thorold*. It was a longer ship than mine, so it took longer to pass their speed-measuring devices. I pointed that out to them, very carefully of course. It's the only time I ever won an argument with the cops."

We have by this time passed through the misty expanse of Lake Ontario overnight; Wolfe Island glimmers grey behind us, the sun burning away early morning mist in the Thousand Islands of the upper St. Lawrence. Then more seaway locks and another set of traffic lights, with gay go up and gay go down, while loudspeakers and computers murmur electronic endearments to each other. An unexpected starling's nest is tucked in the lock wall, where someone must have slipped to allow anything but stone and steel. The mother bird doesn't bat an eyelash as the monster ship gurgles past, home free down the widening river.

On the American side of the seaway, castles of American millionaires are built on green islands, their scores of rooms empty in the late spring season: Heart Island, with battlements and dozens of stone towers, the Boldt Castle, built by a now-dead millionaire. (They die, too, of heart disease and cancer and a great deal of everything, the same way ordinary people do from having too little.) All the limestone and timber components had been hauled in by barge. Farther on, Mary Pickford's castle – she who was America's Sweetheart in the glittering and near-gold heyday of fairyland Hollywood – she who was once a Canadian. And cranes, dozens of the huge birds, rowing through darkening skies to inexpensive tree houses on Ironsides Island.

In many ways the ship is two floating towns, one suburb forward and the other behind. In between are some 450 feet of deck containing the cargo holds. For meals you walk aft to the diningroom, where the crew's cabins and recreation rooms are located, one or two men to each cabin. After dark, streetlights illumine the deck, although I suppose they're called something else. Forward is the officers' quarters, also my own large cabin and bathroom, which fact makes me feel somewhat non-proletarian. There are probably a dozen television sets aboard, and nearly everyone has at least a radio. The meals? Well, the meals are ambrosia and nectar – in fact roast beef, steak, ham, ice cream, the best of everything. Three meat courses for lunch and dinner. Glynn Perry, the First Cook from Roseway, Nova Scotia, could give lessons to a chef at the Queen Elizabeth or Royal York. Leo Riviera, Second Cook, would come first in any culinary contest judged by me.

All these accolades may sound as if I'm being carried away by shipboard luxury. Well, consider this: deckhands are paid between $900 and $1,100 a month, and I don't think that they work very hard, daintily touching up rusted paint-work. For three months in the winter they collect unemployment insurance and drink beer. It occurs to me that I should have known about all this sooner, so that I too could have lived like Mary Pickford and that guy in the Boldt Castle, a middle-aged Croesus happily adding up the interest on my paycheques.

But it is not quite so simple. If not deprivation, there definitely is boredom on board a ship. Leo Riviera says, "You can't see your family for months on end. And what if you need a doctor or dentist in the middle of Lake Ontario? What happens then?"

(Of course, if there's something *really* wrong with you they can get a helicopter by radio-telephone.)

And George Rollier, who is French-French, says, "It's not like being on a deep-sea ship, there's not the same sense of brotherhood and good feeling."

And "Peewee," who is seventeen years old, has decided that after another two or three months, "I'm gone!" One youngster who signed on at Thorold jumped ship between locks at the Welland Canal, perhaps in a sudden frenzy of homesickness. Another deckhand, also from Thorold, de-manded his pay in Baie Comeau at 4 AM, but the Second Mate wouldn't wake Captain Freeman at that hour. Where-upon the discontented seaman jumped ship, stole a milk truck, and drove east until he was picked up by the Quebec Provincial Police at Forestville, seventy miles east.

The *Golden Hind* anchors in the St. Lawrence just below Montreal because of a labour slowdown at Baie Comeau. The stevedores' union there is deliberating about whether the men will go on strike or not. An electrician, nicknamed Freddy Kilowatt, has severe pains in his chest. He is sent to a hospital in the city. And Mike McNulty, one of the young deckhands, has love problems. It seems that there was this girl who liked him much, but he (the cad) brushed her off. She took him at his word and would have no more to do with him, despite prolonged pleading on Mike's part after he discerned the girl's true worth (because of her good judgment in males).

"Will you write me a letter to her?" Mike says, me not having made any secret of being a hack writer.

"Would that be honest?" I ask delicately. "Wouldn't it be love under false pretenses or something?"

"Never mind that. If the letter works, our first child will be named Al."

Okay.

Dear Mary:

I thought of you at the Welland locks, I thought of you anchored below Montreal, and I'll be thinking of you at Tadoussac and Baie Comeau if and when we ever get there. Right now there's a yellow cloud from a factory across the river reflecting itself on the water. It made me think of the yellow rose I gave you, before the ship sailed, to win you back. . . .

"Mike, it's no good. Would any self-respecting, honest-to-goodness, red-blooded Canadian gal go for crap like that ? She sounds too nice to con her, even if I could. I can't do it."

"Yes, you'll have to do better," Mike says judiciously.

"She won't believe it's you!"

"I'll tell her I had help, and besides, the first child will be named –"

"Yes, I know, after me. But the second and third and fourth, what about them?"

"By that time she'll be cussing you so bad you'll hear it in your grave." We stare at each other a moment, and I can see that it is the moment of truth.

"All right, okay," I say to Mike. "I will, in my own inimitable manner and with all the one-syllable words at my command, flatter the hell outa her. What colour hair and eyes?"

After one day near Montreal the *Golden Hind* raised anchor for Ile du Bic, in the St. Lawrence near Rimouski, and there awaited further orders. It's some thirty degrees colder in this area, with still two feet of snow a few miles inland – and it's the beginning of June. Opposite the ship, several miles distant, a string of cottages on the shore looks like stranded icebergs. And just upriver the huge Saguenay River side-swipes the St. Lawrence, marking its passage into the greater river with a five-mile wavery track of foam. On our right – or I should say "starboard" – the freighter *Carol Lake* has been anchored since May nineteenth, also waiting orders for proceeding to Baie Comeau.

Everyone feels very pessimistic about the stoppage. Captain Freeman says it's just for a few days. First Mate Jean Perusse says a week. Glen Smith, the Third Mate, thinks longer than that. Glynn Perry, the First Cook, says gloomily, "We may never leave" I say hell, or even stronger words.

There's lots of time to talk, and Leo Riviera tells me about this friend of his, a deckhand on another ship, who died near Rimouski a few weeks ago. The remains of Tom Beckles were flown back to Barbados via Air Canada, his wife going with him on what was apparently his last journey. But the Canadian authorities hadn't filled in the cause of his death on the death certificate, so back came the body to Canada again. After which, armed with the proper information this time, Beckles and his widow again returned to Barbados.

But there's a prior episode which makes Beckles' death even more poignant for Leo Riviera. "Tom Beckles saved my life. It was in 1941, and I was working on the old Canadian National Steamship, *Lady Hawkins*, as a bellboy. The ship was torpedoed by a German sub off Cape Hatteras, and went down very quickly. There were a lot of people, crewmen and passengers, in the sea before lifeboats could be launched. I was one of them. The water was so cold that it must've weakened me, and I couldn't climb into the boat. I hung onto the gunwale and yelled: 'Tom, help me, help me!' Tom Beckles reached down and hauled me into that lifeboat. There were seventy people in the lifeboat, including my two brothers. One of my brothers died of exposure before we were rescued. That's why I remember Tom Beckles."

And the morning and the afternoon were the second day of boredom, anchored near Ile du Bic in the St. Lawrence. Therefore I called a Royal Commission to investigate the Ontario Paper Company–with myself the only sitting member. (I'd brought along some relevant books for just this purpose.) It seems that Ontario Paper Company owns the Quebec and Ontario Transporation Company, which owns the *Golden Hind*, among other ships, and is itself a subsidiary of many-tentacled American interests, which also include the New York *News* and Chicago *Tribune*. The *Tribune* leads directly to Colonel Robert McCormick. The colonel, who died in 1955, controlled wide stretches of Canadian pulpwood territory at Baie Comeau and Heron Bay, in order to supply raw material for his paper mills, which in turn fed newsprint to the Chicago and New York dailies. And the spoon that fed paper to the US mouth was Ontario Paper Company.

Colonel McCormick is said to be a legendary character. He is credited with being the founding father of the North Shore towns of Shelter Bay (now Port Cartier) and Baie Comeau, and probably deserves it. But with the credit for providing employment must go some small opprobrium, since the country around both settlements, as well as around Heron Bay, is stripped of forest, and nothing meets the eye but rather unlovely underbrush. On the outskirts of Baie Comeau (population some 30,000) is a large canoe made of bronze, with the life-sized colonel sitting inside bolt upright, like a real *Coureur du bois* instead of a newspaper tycoon–no doubt commissioned and paid for by Ontario Paper Company.

Colonel McCormick was not very popular in Canada during the last global conflict. An officer with General "Black Jack" Pershing in the First World War, he became an isolationist in the Second, apparently quite hostile to England,

and *ipso facto* to Canada as well. Thunderous editorials against Britain in the Chicago *Tribune* reflected McCormick's anything-but-neutral views. As a result, a groundswell of public opinion in Canada rose up against his papermaking activities in this country, and newspaper editorials here became quite virulent against the colonel.

Perhaps Napleon Comeau, for whom the town was named, is somewhat more deserving of transient immortal bronze. Before the century's turn, Comeau was a fabulous hunter, trapper, naturalist, and author, who roamed the north Shore performing marvellous feats, rescuing people trapped on ice, and writing books. One of his rescue exploits is depicted on a crest for the new town of Baie Comeau; it is of course, somewhat less expensive than bronze.

One tid-bit of information about papermaking in the nineteenth century, garnered from being the only sitting member on this RoyCom, is fascinating. Newsprint between 1850 and 1860 was made mostly from rags. Thus some newspapers, because of the expense, had to raise their prices to the then-exorbitant ten cents a copy. "Rags were so valuable that enterprising eastern mill operators (presumably in the US) imported shiploads of mummies from Egypt and used the linen wrappings to make paper." Well!–What would Anwar Sadat or defunct Colonel Nasser say about that? Or Moses, who led the Children of Israel out of Egypt? Some of that rag paper made a hundred years ago–could it have been recycled and used again and again? Are we in Canada, perhaps, reading McClelland and Stewart books printed on shiploads of Egyptian mummies?

And the morning and evening were the third day anchored at Ile du Bic. In dreams at night we sailed from boredom to ennui by way of tedium and monotony. The Scotch was all gone, cigars had to be rationed, and "sleep it is a gentle thing, beloved from pole to pole"–but I couldn't court Morpheus without morphia for more than eight hours. And I'd read all my comic books. Lunch and dinner called for long walks aft to the dining room, but still I wasn't getting enough exercise. Pacing off the distance between cabin areas on the central deck of the 620-foot ship, it came to 325 paces for the full circuit, which ought to be around 975 feet if you're fairly tall like myself. Therefore a dozen circuits of the same deck ought to be at least two miles. So I walked two miles every evening. Observing my laudable attempts to keep in shape from deck chairs aft, the First Cook, the Second Cook, and assorted deckhands made inappropriate comments.

"That crummy writer is off his rocker," said Mike.

"He might be just crazy enough to jump overboard," Peewee remarked. Captain Freeman too looked at me slightly askance. I told him I was investigating the possibility that Canadians could walk faster anchored than Swedes could move on bicycles.

And morning and midnight were the seventh day, after which I rose from my bed and walked ashore at Baie Comeau. Orders had come from above to lift anchor aweigh; the stevedores were placated. The ship finally arrived at Napoleon Comeau's town on June eighth. Long steel-girder conveyors unfolded at the dock like praying mantises, sucking up corn and soy beans from the ship's hold amid a man-created storm of dust. A dozen crew members waited to go ashore at the gangplank, all dressed in good non-working clothes and looking strange to me, with a glow of anticipation on their faces. Anticipation for what?

Beer, and more beer, and more beer. The tables were loaded with it. But I couldn't keep up with them. The last I saw of Mike and Peewee was at the pub in Baie Comeau. They waved to me – on their way to more interesting establishments.

During the flight back to Montreal, I kept thinking of that immense river. The St. Lawrence, more than any other, is the River of Canada. You can't row a boat or swim a stroke there without crossing the paths of Jacques Cartier and Samuel de Champlain. Both are basic to what we were and what we have become.

After the long Atlantic journey, then the immigration station at Grosse Isle, newcomers were ferried with muscle and sweat by *batteau* and shank's mare to Lower and Upper Canada. Where there was no beer waiting for them. It is difficult not to think of those people on the river, the dispossessed from France, England, Scotland, and Ireland; difficult because we are their children, and their children's children.

Angus

A long time ago – before most of us were born: 1910. Seventeen-year-old Angus leaned on a fence during moments stolen from schoolwork, watching a fishing boat being built on a stretch of almost deserted beach – the sandy shores of Lake Ontario in Prince Edward County.

For the boy, that boat was a thing of beauty. He pedalled his bicycle there and back home to Trenton every time there was time to watch the boat's water-bound shape afloat on land. The thing stirred young Angus, made his thoughts leap. It was built with hands, the big rough hands of Scott Hutcheson, a fisherman in his tough enduring sixties. It was built with the old manual tools, some having nearly forgotten names, like the adze known to pioneers. It was built with hands.

In the summer of 1968 Angus Mowat walked along that same Lake Ontario beach, as he sometimes did, for exercise and fresh air. Or just from feeling restless. Thinking his own thoughts, he almost stumbled over the derelict, its blurred shape sprouting weeds, and canvas rigging rotted into nowhere. An old fishing boat, washed up by the waves and left there, clothed in an overcoat of yellow sand.

Angus kicked sand away from the near-buried stern with idle curiosity. Derelicts were nothing new on this beach; dinghys and fishing boats drowned continually in paint-blistering sun on the jagged shoreline of Prince Edward County; sometimes he even saw the hundred-year-old timbers of a forgotten windjammer that sailed here, and then sailed by a little-known route into the long silence of sand and sun.

But this boat was different, touching Angus' own memory; a fishing boat that he had seen emerging from someone's mind into physical existence, as he had been growing into being himself after leaving someone else's body.

Scott Hutcheson's boat was hauled from its sand grave to Angus' own backyard. He looked at it: a badly damaged boat. As Angus himself was a damaged human being—his right arm had been badly crippled by high explosive in World War I. Examining the boat brought a mixture of agony and love, a feeling that the past was being turned inside-out; with also the dangerous knowledge that he might be giving way to his own emotions, becoming a silly eccentric old man ? For the dramatic thought was being born that the *Scott Hutcheson* should sail again. (Wow-ie, strike up the band, splice the mainbrace, sound a bugle or two!)

But it was also a sobering thought. For Angus was seventy-six years old, one arm nearly useless, and not a very big man, anyway, to take on all that back-breaking work rebuilding a twenty-nine-foot fishing sloop. Having been a soldier, librarian, and literary gent all his life, he'd never really worked with his hands. But apart from such categories that leave little room in a man's mind for being anything else, Angus was something else.

The old keel, rotting at one end, was removed; clamp after clamp cut with a hacksaw. A new oaken keel, twenty-six feet long, was handhewn with adze and sweat.

"That keel took 27,000 adze strokes," said Angus. "I counted 'em for five minutes, then multiplied that by the hours it took to make the keel, sometimes by guess or by God. But one of us had to be right." Perhaps both of them were, for the new keel fitted into place as if it had never been anywhere else.

The year 1968 became 1969. Summer became winter, and spring forged tiny green jewels on all the trees. Fifty-six narrow oaken ribs were removed from the boat, new ones cut to shape and steamed to proper curvature, then brass-screwed to the planking. The whole job took weeks, because it took all day for two ribs to be installed. Soon it was 1970 and summer again. The rotten planks were extracted, new white cedar planking tapered, steamed, and clamped into place. Elm and maple leaves turned red and fell, as the year turned a corner into autumn.

Boat-building books had to be consulted, of course: but what books say how to build a fishing boat that was born in 1910? Twenty-nine feet long, eight wide, with double-ended lap-strake planking? What authorities are there to measure thought and inches, to calculate stress and strain on a wooden boat whose parts all move in reaction to themselves and the water, each being both themselves and each part of the whole? Who knows that?

One building thought follows another, and the first has to be right or the second dependent thought can't be. An oaken board called a "clamp" runs along the top inside of the boat on both sides. Angus cut that clamp at the wrong angle.

"Maybe I was tired or something. I lived and breathed the boat for such a long time, morning and afternoon and even at night sometimes: maybe I thought it had its own feelings, and a voice would stop me from making mistakes. I was wrong. Weeks and months, and all wasted."

Angus went inside the house, arms tired, brain tired, so discouraged that he wondered if this silly dream was a nightmare, and whether the work of hands that he loved to watch in others was somehow impossible for him. It was early afternoon, the sun spattering the Bay of Quinte with spangles that danced tip-toe on blue waves. Angus had a drink and slept for a couple of hours. His wife, Barbara, made him a sandwich when he woke.

Outside in its canvas shelter, Scott Hutcheson's boat was still stubbornly imperfect, a wooden puzzle into which one of the parts refused to fit. Over Angus' shoulder in the late afternoon sun a voice said, "Awful isn't it?"—musingly, as if someone had been watching Angus work with sympathy, but no hint of condescension. Scott Hutcheson himself, of course. Angus knew that. Scott Hutcheson, who'd spent his life as a fisherman and then died. "Take that clamp out and do it again," Scott said.

"All right, then," Angus said, "I will."

How many of us living here and now hear voices from the past ? "Dammit," said Angus, "I knew he was there! In my mind, in the earth, in the water, and all around me. Don't tell me I'm crazy, I know that already. But Scott knew I needed help, because after all he did have some small interest in the reconstruction of what had been something nearly perfect, the shape of a boat married to water. Or thought married to substance, if you want to call it that."

The Trenton of young Angus Mowat and old Scott Hutcheson at the century's turn was a town where everything moved slowly. Streets were dirt with farm wagons and buggies clopping down the road on market days, raising a smoky dust. Bells on horses' harnesses jingled in winter, and there was the crunch-crunch of your feet on dry snow like regular heartbeats. Loungers leaned against the Gilbert Hotel on the main street, chewing tobacco, watching things slowly happen with dispassionate and rather superior interest. There were no streetlights. Buildings were lit with coal-oil lamps. When electricity first thrilled through the houses and blazed outside, the birds didn't know what to think.

Trenton was my town as well as Angus' town. I grew up there, too, twenty-five years after he did. Which is how I happen to know the way it was. What I didn't know then was that everything was about to change; the slow clop-clop of a small town's heart would soon speed up to a gallop, the horses mostly die and be replaced by tractors and motor cars. Maybe that's not bad. It had to happen. Just the same, it was a different morning then. On one of them I came down the stairs on tip-toe so I wouldn't wake my mother, closed the screen door softly, and crossed a dirt road to the river, my part-airedale dog following like a dog-shadow behind. There's something uncanny in thinking about doing this so long afterwards:

Blacksmiths are, of course, necromancers and wizards. Angus knew this and so did I. We watched the cherry-red iron shoes glow and smelled the sweet-sickening odor of horses' hooves together and apart from our twenty-five-year interval of being there. The blacksmith's name was C.P. Yourex.

If you don't know how things are done, made, manufactured, it's a mysterious process to watch happening for the first time. The pumpmaker's shop was a dark dusty cave, full of strong scent of pine and cedar. Wheels turned and belts whirred. Enthralled boys crowded the doorway to watch—but timidly, for old MacLean's temper was an uncertain quantity. Sometimes he would grunt beneath his yellow beard, and chase Angus and me and the other boys off home with a terrifying yell. We never knew if it was real anger or only play-acting.

In winter with red scarves coiled around our cold noses we'd watch the sleighs coming upriver from the Bay of Quinte, each piled high with three-foot chunks of ice. The great horses' hooves beat on their ice road in heavy rhythm to match the zero-zero sound of bells. When the smoke-breathing teams stopped, we watched their crystal cargo conveyed along rollers to the sawdusty icehouse, horses doing the hauling and teamsters yelling "Giddyup" or "Whoa" in voices like thunder. Angus and I never knew exactly where that ice came from, until we snitched a ride on the sleighs one cold day, and watched the elemental stuff being sawed like lumber and magicked off to the housewives' town.

"Angus," I say, "was it like that for you as it was for me?"

"Until the war. Then everything changed. I was a kind of Victorian prig before that."

"What about the war?"

"I don't want to talk about the war."

"Look, I'm doing this piece about you. Don't be so damn difficult."

"Well (a little surlily), whaddaya wanta know?"

Angus dreams still of World War I. The Fourth Battalion marches and counter-marches in his head, all in vivid colour. One scrap of the rarely-talked-about reality: after being a private for fourteen months, Angus was commissioned in the field as a second looey. His Uncle Jack Mowat was a major in the Somme battle sector. At the same time there was this Sergeant Crouch who had a yen for souvenirs—always laden down with German turnip watches and helmets in the Regina Trench.

Comes attack and counter-attack by the enemy, and ground hard-won by Canadian troops is lost. Then with shells bursting and bullets whining, the Fourth Battalion retakes the Regina Trench. But Uncle Jack Mowat was wounded in one arm and is missing. Where is he now? Find him, says the CO. Sergeant Crouch and Second-Looey Angus go out to search: but there is nothing to find. Major Mowat had been blown apart, his body completely disintegrated. His soul? Maybe it screamed for a few seconds where his body had been, hovering over a lost place in the Regina Trench on the Somme.

Angus was Major Angus in World War II, no longer a member of the Fourth Battalion, but the newly formed Hastings and Prince Edward Regiment—a staff officer this time.

"I was old," says Angus defensively. "And my right arm war nearly useless after the first war."

Long after the last of all our wars an echo of the Hasty P's regimental marching song is still heard sometimes at the armoury parade-ground in Belleville:

From the town of Napanee
Came a horse's ass—that's me,
Where my father shovelled horseshit on the street.
And one day late in the fall
He found me among the balls,
So he picked me up and called me
Hasty P—

After World War I Angus was a beekeeper, a fire ranger, and worked briefly in a sash and door factory. In 1924 he became librarian at Trenton. Says Angus: "It was known that I had once read a book." In the late thirties he wrote two of them himself, both novels: *Then I'll Look Up* (1939) and *Carrying Place* (1941). His son also writes.

Angus reorganized the libraries at Trenton, Belleville, Windsor, and Saskatoon before World War II. In 1937 he was appointed Director of Ontario Public Libraries. "I loved the work" he says. "People and books are the most important things in life."

"Angus, what is there about living in a small town at the turn of the nineteenth century?"

Angus has a full white beard, which he fondly imagines makes him look like a Highland Scot. He waved it at me thoughtfully. "Everyone was going to live forever; we all knew that. A boy could believe what older people told him, then. A man might be digging ditches, at the bottom of what you might call the social strata: but always in his mind he knew that he was a relative of the chief. No, not nobility, something more important—the feeling that you were known or even loved sometimes by everyone in that small town."

I mentioned dryly to Angus that my memory of Trenton held no such vision of inherent natural nobility. "You were a sonuvabitch even then," he said calmly. Of course, you have to be a bit cautious with Angus, flattery must be acid-coated and you get in another remark quickly before the beard waggles like a major or a library inspector or a literary gent. Angus is not exactly a gentleman of the old school, either, mannered and courtly. He bites.

We are sitting in Angus' livingroom under the high-arched ceiling, drinking brandy slowly, and slowly words die down. Barbara and my wife are preparing dinner. The fireplace stirs, red coals and grey ash about to collapse on itself. It seems almost idyllic—a nice prettied-up picture of human existence. Hence I feel I've missed something, left something out.

Maybe after a long life that is crowded with shame and pride, adventure and monotony, what a man is becomes clear finally through where he is, how he talks, what goods and chattels he owns—all part of the total bundle of Angus. In my own worst moments many people seem to me to be only talking heads, pre-programmed to speak all the words inherited from the faraway grunts and moans of a million years of human ancestry. Speech is dubbed-in by fathers and mothers, the deliberate teaching of sound symbols and the intuitive gestures of hand and body that we all inherit. And then the people who went before disappear at some point in our lives into empty space behind us. It must be done like that, of course, for there is no other way.

But then there's Scott Hutcheson's boat and its three years of re-building, with no power tools used; its subtle anachronistic design, in which the stern bolts are so arranged that no propellor can ever be installed—like a chastity belt against the machine age. For me that boat is a survival from the past, just as an unborn baby's swift progression through all the previous animal stages before the triumph of being born is such a survival. It speaks for all the Greek triremes and Roman galleys, dromonds and hollowed-out logs and Egyptian barges that rot and rot forever at the mouth of the Trent or some other nameless river in the Mediterranean basin. It speaks for Angus.

Sipping the brandy slowly (Barbara frowns from the kitchen), Angus says, "The lines of that boat are as near perfection as a man or a boat can get. The only one of its kind left on the Bay of Quinte."

"Continuity and survival?" I say, unsubtly insistent. The beard waggles at me. He knows I know he knows.

But only yesterday Scott Hutcheson had the last word: "That deck beam is all wrong. It ain't worth a pinch of coonshit!"

96

Seven-League Skates:
An Interview with Brian Glennie

What is it that symbolizes Canada to itself, the sort of thing known by most Canadians from one end of the country to the other? A list might include the CBC, beavers, Mounties, the maple leaf, John Diefenbaker–and certainly hockey. There are more than 600,000 league players in Canada (compared to 6,000,000 in Russia); by all odds this pastime of glorified shinny on ice is the one that Canadians can be most passionate about.

Hockey was invented in Canada, either at Montreal or at Kingston, some 120 years ago. Certain basic myths have developed about it, in the same way that the Ty Cobb and Babe Ruth myths became part of baseball south of the border. Cyclone Taylor (said to have scored a goal while skating backwards), Newsy Lalonde, Joe Malone, and many others are part of it. But the primeval myth is a success story: the big-league scout combing the sticks for talent, sitting in a smoky small-town rink without artificial ice, watching the local flash, himself watched in turn by local cognoscenti, who are fascinated to see this representative of sudden riches smoking a cigar as if he were human. The young local flash signs a contract for much money, makes good with the big team and returns to marry his childhood sweetheart. Sometimes the youngster's name turns out to be Bobby Hull, Gordie Howe, Rocket Richard, or Bobby Orr. We all knew it could happen for the myth is based on reality.

The basics of hockey precede present-day machine-made players, drilled into excellence by endless practice and by reiterated advice from coaches. It goes beyond artificial ice, back to the toddling tykes learning to skate on lakes and rivers and backyard ponds. You can still see them there, batting an old tin can or rock between two baskets that simulate a goaltender's net. I was one of them myself years ago, bundled up in windbreaker and scarf, wearing old-fashioned double-bladed skates, face raw with cold. I remember that there was always one kid better than the rest, a kid who could take a lump of coal and stickhandle it through a whole crowd of other youngsters trying to stop him. And sometimes, when the river ice was clear of snow, the game would occupy acres and acres of ice, occasionally even flowing out from the Trent River and onto the huge Bay of Quinte among the far-away fishing shanties, with slow clouds lifting ahead like giant goalies. You could race over miles and miles of ice with twenty-foot strides on seven-league skates: you were the next thing to immortal and only ten years old. Then stop and look down at the black ice, seeing this kid with a red nose, suddenly aware of the difference between body and watching mind, himself observing himself.

Brian Glennie is a solid 200 pound thirty-year-old defenseman with the Toronto Leafs, a blueline basher and a hammer made of flesh. But not a star. I've seen Brian miss a bodycheck sometimes and look rather foolish. Once he bounced a pass off the referee's skate; it was picked up by an opposing forward, who scored easily. The Leafs lost again. They'd been losing endlessly at the time—three weeks without a win. But around four years previously, when his team was also playing badly, it seemed to me that Glennie pulled them out of the slump with his checking, almost singlehandedly. He stood up straight at the blueline, delivering clean classic checks, hip and shoulder whomping opposing players so hard that they sustained damage to both rump and ego; a player reminiscent of previous Leaf body thumpers like Bucko McDonald, Bingo Kampman, and Red Horner (notice those lusty nicknames!), bashers who hit so hard that they sometimes broke their own or the other guy's suspenders. If they missed, spectators in the front-row seats caught cold from the draft. They are also reminiscent of myself, playing pick-up hockey at age seventeen; a 180-pound stringbean, I'd try to hit like Red Horner and nearly always miss. I quit shortly after that, from shame at my own ineptitude.

I suppose that's why I wanted to talk to Brian Glennie, a quiet guy who has to work harder than most players, skating a little slower than the blinding speedsters, wearing this droopy moustache that gives him a mournful look. We drank some beer while I tried to get him off the subject of the Leafs' three-week losing streak.

"When you're losing," Brian says, "winning is everything. There's no joy in the game, not when you're losing. But don't get me wrong—I love hockey. I eat, sleep, and drink the game. So if the Leafs ever start to win, I'll start feeling human again. But right now I'm liable to go home and hear Barb say, 'Let's go out tonight.' But I don't wanta go out. Someone would be sure to say to me, 'what's wrong with the Leafs, Brian?' Or, 'I hear you're gonna be traded to another team.'"

Every time I try to switch the subject from losing and Brian's depression, he comes back to it as inevitably as a homing pigeon.

"It's gotten so bad that I say to myself," he says, "look; Brian, you've got an education—Bachelor of Arts in psychology and two years of physical education at the University of

Toronto—so you could go back to school and get the hell outa hockey for good. Because it's stopped being fun. The only reason for playing during the last three weeks is money."

Well, he's even got me depressed by now. But then I'm a Leafs' fan from way back.

One night in January, 1975, I watched the Leafs play the Washington Capitals, a last-place expansion team, in Maple Leaf Gardens. I'm sitting in the gold seats near rinkside with Dick Beddoes, who's probably the best sports writer in Canada. Outside on the street scalpers, who hawk tickets at exorbitant prices to last-minute arrivals, can't sell them. Inside what Dick calls "the sports centre of Canada," floodlights blaze down and hockey players swing back and forth in the pre-game warm-up. Sixteen thousand people buzz conversation; the press gallery is crowded.

"The Caps are the worst team in hockey," Dick says, "at least the worst team in the National League. The Leafs ought to win by six goals."

"What if they don't?"

"Don't ask that—Harold Ballard is a sick man!"

The players glide across the ice easily and gracefully as swans, betraying no skills except skating. Some are in red Washington sweaters, other in the Leafs' white and blue: a blaze of colour. Nothing that you see on television equals it, for this TV screen is as wide as a city block, this noise is not electronic. Of course, the men are playing a children's game, arrested in semi-permanent childhood until retirement and the beginnings of a pot-belly. But the game is definitely glamorous, for here the myth of hockey is perpetuated: the myth that says Canadians are the best hockey players in the world, from which we derive national ego-sustenance, as necessary as mother's milk. And the kids coming up from smoky small-town arenas—where they used to open side windows in the days before artificial ice so that the rinks could freeze—those kids know that this brightly-lit arena is their goal, mecca of all their hopes for glory and money – not necessarily in that order of importance. Claire Alexander, the thirty-one-year-old Leaf rookie who was delivering milk in a small town two years back, knows it, too. My friend, Dick Beddoes, originally a Vancouver sports writer who rejected offers from American newspapers in order to come to Toronto, also knows that this is the Big Apple, Hogtown Toronto.

"Will you sign my program, Mr. Beddoes?" a ten-year-old voice pipes close to my ear.

"Of course," Dick says, "what's your first name?" The kid glows.

A few minutes later, with the Leafs short-handed because of a penalty, Lanny McDonald gets too fancy stickhandling with the puck, losing it inside his own blueline. A Washington player picks it up and, BOOM, he scores. It's one to nothing for the Caps. Omigawd, here we go again! Three weeks losing, let's make it four!

"Doesn't matter," Dick says, "we'll get it back." (He has faith!) The Leafs look bad. Their passing is lousy. Glennie missed a bodycheck, and nobody can put two things together long enough to make them add up to one. Jim McKenny, the Leafs' slick defenceman, crashes into the boards, and I can see an expression of pain on his face that the TV camera doesn't. He leaves the ice for repairs and rest. Kids' treble voices shriek, "Come on Leafs! Come on Leafs!" Hesitantly, sluggishly perhaps, the Leafs do start to come. They score. They score again. The kids are ecstatic, they are all believers. Darryl Sittler slides beautifully through the whole Washington team in the second period, and scores while upsidedown in front of the net.

A scrimmage in front of the Leafs' goal: Doug Favell, the goalie, crashes painfully into the post, and squirms in non-phony technicolour agony. He seems hurt badly when they help him off the ice. Of course we win – I mean Leafs win – 7-1. And the ex-milkman, Claire Alexander, also scores a flukey goal from the point (the place inside the blueline where an attacking player is stationed to make either a pass or a slapshot). Anyway, the Leafs gave the puck to Alexander, his first and maybe his only goal in the big leagues.

At game's end Dick Beddoes has signed some twenty-five programs, mostly for kids. I realize, with slight surprise, that my friend is famous: fifteen of his autographs equal one Bobby Orr.

Dick and I talk to Red Kelly, the Leafs' coach. Kelly is forty-six; calm and measured in manner; his strongest cuss-word is "By hang." Then we go to the dressing room where the players are in various stages of undress. These nude heroes show what a difference uniforms make. Cowboy Bill Flett is tremendously muscled, but the other supermen seem ordinary. Dick chats with Doug Favell , who'd been replaced by Dunc Wilson after his encounter with the goal post. The injury hadn't been serious; some kind of muscle spasm that he shook off fairly easily. The goalie appears small without his bulky pads, yet weighs about 175 pounds. Darryl Sittler, scoring star for the Leafs, looks like a high school youngster. Dave Keon, team veteran of many years, talks to Dick about the Leafs' long losing streak. He makes the point that kids crawl before they learn to walk, just as rookie players must learn to work hard, and it takes time for the component parts of a team to come together. I've seen accountants who looked and talked like Keon. Yet this is the man who sometimes won't talk to the press at all, because he feels so savagely bad when the Leafs lose.

Glennie, like Keon, feels slightly better over the Leafs' win – but he's not turning any handsprings about it. The game is life and death to him, as well as bread and butter. Brian tells me about his wife, Barbara, being in hospital earlier in the season.

"She was gonna have a big operation for a pelvic abcess. I couldn't even think about hockey at the time. Now, if I'd been in any ordinary line of work, I'd have been at my wife's side when she had that operation. All right, so what do I do? I stay at the Gardens and play hockey that night.

Sure, I condemn myself for it! She was on the operating table for three hours, she could've died! I think, what if it's all over for Barb? I'm on the ice playing a lousy game while that's happening. I mean, what really are the priorities of life? What bugged me was that it would never enter into my mind to go to the coach and say, 'Hey, my wife's on the operating table, I want to go to the hospital!' And Kelly would have said go ahead, I know he would."

"But you didn't do that?"

"No, I played hockey."

"Why didn't you go?"

"I don't know, maybe it's because I'm conditioned, a conditioned hockey player. I didn't even think to ask."

Quiet, red-haired Barbara says of that operation, "It would have been nice to have Brian there. I mean, I was really sick. But hockey comes first, life is pushed aside."

"Do you want him to retire and get another job?"

"I want Brian to do what he wants to do, I guess that means playing hockey, but again, that's up to him. Of course, hockey was exciting at first—being married to someone so well-known—but now it's a drag."

Barb is twenty-nine; she grew up in Oshawa. She says that she always wanted to get married and have kids. She likes being a woman. "Sure—it's nice to have doors opened for you, and be treated as someone special." But she doesn't go to hockey games. Wife Barbara and husband Brian live lives so different and separate that Barb's interests—painting and modern dance—are alien to him. "Brian isn't interested in my painting or dancing, I can tell. But we do have a good relationship."

Brian is as obsessive about his wife's operation as he is about the losing Leafs. "After it was over, I talked to Andrea Kelly (the coach's wife). She told me about having an emergency appendix operation a few years ago. Red had to rush her to the hospital, find someone to look after the kids, go play hockey himself, then come back and see her. The same thing as Barb went through and I went through. And who in hell, the rest of his life, would be as spellbound by a game as that?"

There's a kind of agony in all this that I didn't quite expect. Of course, hockey players are human beings like everyone else. I knew that; but the sports pages rarely mention such things; and to the treble-voiced kids, pain and suffering happen to their mothers and dads, not to their heroes' wives. What it amounts to is: men playing a children's game, but forced to be adults in their private lives, forced to look at themselves squarely as human beings, prone to human as well as athletic errors.

In 1952 at age six, Brian Glennie was a boy playing a boy's game with the Marlboros of the Little Toronto Hockey League. The stocky kid with the determined look had the same coach many kids have, his father. Alex Glennie went to the rink with him sometimes; the thirty-seven-year-old employee of Shell Oil cheered Brian on from the sidelines.

"Even in those days, I was generally a little better than most kids," says Brian. But that was before he started playing with the big boys, like Bobby Orr, Gordie Howe, Robert Marvin Hull—and the quicksilver Russians. In high school he went out for basketball, football, and gymnastics, joining the Marlboro Junior A hockey team in 1964. By that time Glennie was a heavily built defenceman, who could sometimes score a few goals for you—but a little slow for the National League, according to pro scouts. Brian made up that deficiency by being in the right place at the right time, and in 1967 his Marlboros won the Memorial Cup and were junior hockey Champions of Canada. That's the supreme pinnacle for any team, for junior A's (age twenty-one and under) are the coddled bluebloods of hockey, many of them future professionals. The junior A's are the seedbed and breeding ground of pro hockey. For a brief time, all the hockey fans in Canada look squarely at you. It's a time when the back-slapping, fulsome praise and the "You're lookin' great, kid!" kind of talk begins.

Alexander Glennie died of a heart attack at age fifty-two, the same year the Marlboros nabbed the silver trinket that means the junior supremacy of Canada. Brian was knocked out with grief and loss. He had always depended on his father for advice. When the older Glennie said, "Get an education!", Brian went to University of Toronto in 1967. There he met pretty red-haired Barbara Holland from Oshawa, who was also doing a physical education course. After discussing plans with his mother, Irene Glennie, a lawyer's secretary, and Barb, Brian joined the National Team at Winnipeg, which was coached by Father Bauer, and enrolled at the University of Manitoba.

The year 1968 was an Olympic year, and the Canadian team was supposed to win, according to coach Bauer. But surprise, the Finns beat them; they struggled to a win over the United States, then beat Czechoslovakia and Sweden, reaching the final against Russia with the world amateur title almost within their grasp. Says Brian, "Motivating yourself is easy when you play for your country. When the national anthem begins, everybody is higher than a kite!" But kites come down: Canada lost 5-0 to Russia, finishing third in the final standings.

Brian signed with the Leafs in May of 1968, got married in 1969, and there are now two kids, Rebecca and Adam. Injuries began to be a problem after turning pro. He's had two shoulder operations, both legs and ankles in casts, ribs separated, nose broken a few times, and countless facial cuts requiring multiple stitches. In 1972 his right shoulder was damaged, and he had to be fitted with a special harness in order to play hockey. He couldn't lift his right arm above the shoulder. "Every time I was hit in a game my arm would dislocate, then go back into place." That harness had to be worn till after Christmas, then "I hit somebody along the boards, heard this tremendous snap, and went out like a light."

Glennie woke up in the hospital, leg and ankle both in a plaster cast. The doctors wanted to operate on his shoulder as well, since he was already in the hospital, but "I said Whoa! Later I went back into the hospital and had the shoulder operated on. But I just couldn't take both the leg and shoulder operations at the same time." Brian says about playing while in pain, "If it hurts like hell I'm not gonna tell you anyway! You know – I may think I'm dying, but I'm gonna go back out there!" Is such courage heroic, or just foolish?

In 1972 Glennie was a member of Team Canada – a non-playing member – but it was the big emotional experience of his life. "You know, it was unbelievable, the lengths that the Russians went to off the ice to bother our hockey club – to upset both players and wives. But when we came off the ice in Moscow at the end of the second period with the series itself tied, and with Canada behind 5-3 in the final game, the feeling in that dressing room was electric. Everybody knew that there was no way the Russians were going to beat us! Why not? I don't know, but we knew!"

The Russians played for a tie when the score was 5-5, but then Paul Henderson scored a last-minute winning goal and all was bedlam. Afterwards Henderson said, "When I scored that final goal, I finally realized what democracy was all about."

Brian said, "Eventually it *did* become a matter of democracy versus communism." Is that what playing the national anthem does?

Now, after many years with the Leafs, Brian Glennie is a veteran, wondering what it's all about: "My brain is rotting from disuse ever since I left university." Barbara is developing her own interests: "Her life can't simply revolve around mine, much as I'd like that." About his own play: "I've learned nothing since I turned pro. Sometimes I wonder why you can't place a video camera at one end of the rink to watch the way Bobby Orr comes in on the defense. Orr is the greatest player I've ever seen. Does he go to the right or left in a stress situation, and how many times?" Such confrontations, which happen several times in a game, are the real magic of hockey – one man meeting two defensemen at the blueline, then, miraculously, he's around or between them. After the fact, nobody knows how it was done; most of the time pictures don't explain it. So it's ballet, it's murder, it's the reason why men play a boy's game despite pain and regardless of the money. And we who watch, and who were never good enough to play ourselves, can admire the pure wizardry of the game at its best, applauding madly and wondering at our own foolish joy.

At the end of all our talk, I have this vision of slow lumbering Brian Glennie, blueline basher, booming body hitter non-extraordinaire, he with the Maple Leaf tattooed on his backside. In my vision Glennie is sleeping, he is also dreaming. His moustache quivers with the force of missed body-checks in his dream of hockey. The slick quicksilver attackers skate all around him, laughing, jeering at his inability to stop them. They fill the Leafs' net with goals. The score is 50 to 1 against. It doesn't matter, Brian still keeps missing body-checks, and they still keep laughing. The score is now 100 to zero against (the first score was an error). Brian's moustache quivers some more with frustration; he sobs brokenly in his sleep; Barb is alarmed and thinks of waking him. The moustache is a barometer of things, it crackles electrically. Then, suddenly (WOW!) Brian nails one of those smartass enemy forwards, hits him so hard the opposing goaltender's suspenders snap in sympathy. And you know what happens? Well, the guy is well and truly nailed. So the other enemy skaters have to keep their heads up from caution. They start missing passes and get confused. All the little kids rise up in their seats and yell with treble voices, "Come on, Leafs!" Pretty soon the score is 101 to 100, Leafs ahead. The bell goes, Brian smiles in his sleep, all the little kids cheer like mad, Barb sighs a little, and life is so simple if you win. Like Brian says, winning is everything? Not quite, but it does make you think and wonder about all the other important things.

Norma, Eunice, and Judy

Canada?," I've heard it said, "why, there's no such place!" A non-country, the only western so-called nation to have its 1936 Olympic athletes give Hitler the Nazi salute. A kind of vacuum between parentheses. The sort of place where anyone with the least vestige of ability leaves quickly to avoid contamination by their fellow nonentities. An outlying colony of Imperial America, bought and paid for by the United States – if not yet signed, sealed, and delivered to them. A nation without culture, art, or literature: a 4,000-mile-wide chunk of Arctic desert: a Mobius strip facing the United States and turning away from itself uneasily because there is really no self to verify its own existence.

That's what many people think of Canada, including Canadians. It leaves the youngsters who are going to school here and just beginning to think for themselves in a terrible quandary. They ask themselves the old question "Who am I?" – then look around to discover that none of their schoolmates know, either; in fact, neither do many adult Canadians. And yet, incongruously, inside the vacuum a ground-swell of nationalism is making itself felt–Nationalism as the knowledge that we are here, and reality begins here. For reality is what you can touch and feel in the areas immediately beyond your eyes, and in the space that surrounds your body. It is the consciousness of self as the last link in a long line of selves, a knowledge of what those others did in the past before the present self fades and rejoins the past.

But what if there is actually no knowledge–or very little–of our own reality in the present-past? Or none beyond a dead parade of events that recorded history does not bring to life–the record of occupied space and time without purpose or meaning? What does our young student in a Canadian secondary school feel then, in a country where the native literature is added to English Literature or American Literature like an afterthought? Where it is said to be not worth teaching? Who shall he turn to then? How shall he answer that question, "Who am I?" To whom can he turn for knowledge of Canadian literature?

There is really only one man: Jim Foley of Port Colborne, a high school teacher who has seen his own interest in Canadian writing balloon from personal enjoyment and spare-time passion to a lifelong, whole-hearted obsession. A mild-mannered, balding man in his early fifties, Foley says, "I guess I didn't know what was happening to me. I just got involved more or less gradually. But when I realized that Canada must be the only country in the world where high school kids aren't taught their own literature, then I had to tell them and their teachers about it. I had to tell them what they're missing!"

This spinning globe has a fair number of obsessed people walking around on it, even a few grinding their own axes in the interests of education. Jim Foley, with his wife and four children, his job teaching at the local high school–even with the recurrent coronaries that will probably kill him eventually–does not seem unusual. The way he walks and talks seems to say that high drama is for the athletes (although he was a football and hockey player during his own schooldays), drama is for Moses or Moishe Dayan or Richard Nixon: "I'm a teacher." And yet this is the man who, after an experimental CanLit course in Brantford in 1966, organized Port Colborne's Canada Day in 1971 and every year thereafter, which nearly every writer of any prominence in the country has attended, donating their services for free.

Canada Day in March, 1974, came off just after Jim Foley had his last heart attack; a mild one this time, no big deal, he says. But organizing the affair with its several dozen writers in attendance, along with visitors from outside, students of Port Colborne High School, Secretary of State Hugh Faulkner, and Mel Hurtig among the guests, and financing by the Canada Studies Foundation and the local mayor and chamber of commerce and Foley himself – all this calls for a driving man, maybe even a prophetic, vituperative Moses totally unlike the stricken image of Foley himself.

"It will come," he says in his non-Moses voice. "A few years from now, perhaps, but it will come. Margaret Laurence, Atwood, Layton, Garner, and all the others who talk about the place we live in, their voices will be heard and taught in our schools. Those writers are the people who dream for students, kind of like springboards from which the kids' own thoughts can leap somewhere else."

In the meantime Foley and his wife answer a thousand letters a month from all over Canada, mostly from teachers who want to teach CanLit, but don't know anything about it. In the meantime he fires off letters to Thomas Wells, Ontario Minister of Education, urging that CanLit be taught. In almost non-existent spare time he is compiling an Information Bank on Canadian books – 7,000 of them – cross-indexing by topic: ethnic groups, cities, the Depression, women's rights, etc., etc.

He collects beer bottles with his students and shows movies to raise money for the annual Canada Day, as well as lecturing wherever anyone wants him to go, wheedling, coaxing, temporizing, and soliciting funds whenever anyone shows signs of interest. All this activity is a little like the mole that began moving a mountain mouthful by mouthful, then found that the mountain had a heart of stone.

Jim Foley was born in 1922. Both his parents died when he was four, so the youngster ended up in an orphanage, which he hated. He ran away from it at age nine, roaming the streets of Toronto's Cabbagetown, stealing apples and oranges from fruit stores, sleeping wherever he could find a warm place, running away from whoever was chasing him, whether cops or skid-row bums.

At 269 Carlton, just down the street from Maple Leaf Gardens, was a house that wasn't a home in 1932. Young Foley wandered into it looking for shelter, for food, looking for something. Three prostitutes who lived there adopted the boy unofficially. They fed and clothed him, sent him to school, wiped his nose, and made him do his homework. And gave him love: "No mother could have loved me more than those three," says Jim Foley. Their names were Norma, Eunice, and Judy. Hallowed be their names!

I don't know what to call 269 Carlton Street: was it a brothel, a house of ill-fame, or a whorehouse? At any rate, it was a home for Jim Foley from age nine onwards. He washed the floors and helped with the dishes. When he had a cold, Norma, Eunice, and Judy nursed him, tucked him into bed, told him bedtime stories. A few years later they paid his way to St. Michael's College, where he played football and hockey. Teammates at St. Mike's were Nick Metz, Pep Kelly, Art Jackson, and Roy Conacher; the first three playing for the Toronto Leafs after junior hockey, always slightly in the shadow of the "Kid Line" of Busher Jackson, Joe Primeau, and Charlie Conacher during the Leafs' great days—the days of hockey heroes, the days when some of us are old enough now to have been young then. And in the gondola at Maple Leaf Gardens, down the street from 269 Carlton, Foster Hewitt shrieked into the radio microphone: "He shoots, he scores!"

But Jim Foley never scored. He was just too small, only 115 pounds soaking wet. But his days of wandering the streets of Cabbagetown, stealing fruit from Ciro's at the corner of Carlton and Parliament, swimming skinny in the Don River, being chased by conductors after pulling the trolley wires off street cars—those days were over. He went to Columbia University in New York instead, and became, he says, "a professional student" rather than a pro hockey player. Financed, of course, by Norma, Eunice, and Judy.

Twenty years later Jim Foley challenged Canadian writers, publishers, and educators during a Canada Day panel discussion on what he called "the apathy about Canadian Literature in this country." The little high school teacher, a mouse among the elephants, daring the Deputy Minister of Education for Ontario, George Waldrum, and other assorted big-wigs to contradict him, told about people being stopped on the streets of large cities two years ago and asked to name five Canadian writers. "Of the over one hundred people stopped, none could give five names." Which sounded like an accusation, and it was. "I looked through bookstores in Hamilton and Niagara Falls a while back," Foley added, then paused. "You know what I found, or rather what I did not find? On the shelves of those bookstores, zero to one per cent of the books were Canadian."

Somebody said "Harumphh"—maybe it was the Deputy Minister of Education—then, placatingly, that there was a need for a few more Port Colbornes in this country, in which case there would be no problem with apathy about Canadian literature. Publisher Jack Stoddart denied apathy entirely, mentioning as proof the 3,000 people in attendance at Canada Day. Novelist Hugh Garner said Canadian literature was just coming into its own. Poet Don Gutteridge felt likewise. Others too denied the charge.

If something is said vigorously, attacked vigorously, people will always be found to take the opposite viewpoint. The elephant's tail switches angrily at his tormenter, but the mouse is smiling. And no one could refute the charge that only zero to one per cent of the books in most of our bookstores were Canadian. And those one hundred people stopped on the street who couldn't name five authors—how many of some 23,000,000 Canadians could do any better? Or, reversing the question, could five authors contain in their writings the hopes and aspirations of 23,000,000 Canadians?

I asked Jim Foley, "What happened after you went to New York? What about those three surrogate mothers in Cabbagetown?"

"They wrote me a letter after I had spent two years at Columbia. They said that it's best we shouldn't see each other any more. They said: "It's better that way, now that you are at university and will amount to something, it's better that way.' "

"Did you ever see them again?"

"I went back to the house on Carlton Street, but couldn't find them."

"Everything else the way it was, exactly the same house?"

"Yes, but only strangers answered the door."

While at university, Foley worked as an orderly at a New York hospital and as a part-time janitor. He received athletic scholarships to play hockey and football, leaving Columbia with a PhD in Philosophy. After working in Japan during the Korean War, he taught high school in Rivers, Manitoba, in Sioux Lookout and then Brantford, and finally in Port Colborne; getting married in 1952, then the children.

In 1974 Foley is sitting in his office, cross-indexing 7,000 Canadian books, answering letters from teachers and kids, saying "Dear Mr. Suchandsuch: Yes, Hugh Garner writes about Cabbagetown in Toronto (I know it well). W. O. Mitchell writes about the Prairies, Jake and the Kid, and Crocus, Sask. Margaret Laurence about Manawaka. But don't let that fool you, Manawaka is really Neepawa, Manitoba. And there is Ernest Buckler in the Annapolis Valley, Hugh MacLennan in Nova Scotia, and Quebec with its 'Two Solitudes.' Yes, they are real places. Yes, they are home-country. . . ."

Poets in Montreal

In October, 1955, I landed at Irving Layton's house at Côte St. Luc in Montreal, en route to Europe. Curt Lang, a friend, was already there, and had been given the studio couch for a bed. Myself, the late-comer, had to be satisfied with the livingroom floor. Irving and Betty Layton welcomed us warmly; the kids, Maxie and Cissie-Bou (her real name was Naomi), taking Curt and me for soft touches, immediately demanded nickels. Irving himself had a personality like an attractive bulldozer, and few could resist his charm when he wanted to turn it on. He was about forty-two at that time, with a physique something like Two-Ton Tony Galento, a heavyweight fighter of the day whom probably no one now remembers. Betty was fresh-faced and smiled easily, a painter of more than ordinary talent.

The prelude to this meeting with Layton began a year or so earlier in Vancouver. In 1954, when I was working at a Vancouver mattress factory, I came across a review of Irving Layton's poems in a literary magazine. The review was favourable, so I wrote to Layton and ordered a couple of his books. Curt Lang and I read the poems with amazed delight, for Layton dispensed with all the good-breeding and politeness of other Canadian poets and critics of that time. I soon got into a correspondence with Irving, and not long after that was canvassing Vancouver book stores on his behalf, trying to have them stock Layton's books.

I was thirty-four years old then, and had just discovered T.S. Eliot (although I didn't like him much) and Dylan Thomas. (Certain good friends have been unkind enough to suggest that I was retarded.) By 1955, Curt Lang had pretty well brainwashed me into believing that I was a writer. He admired my poems, and few can resist that. I admired his poems, which he didn't resist much, either. After five years at Vancouver Bedding, I'd become exceedingly unpopular with management, since I'd helped to unionize the place. I hated going to work from eight to five every day so badly that I felt death might be preferable.

So there I was, pretending to be a writer, on my way to Europe in 1955. I couldn't back out now, for I was sure to get fired because of the union, even if I wanted to stay at the factory. In the midst of this identity-crisis, I wasn't at all sure what a writer was or whether I might be one.

I landed on Layton's doorstep and eventually on his floor that morning in October, feeling like a ghost in transit from life to death. For by now I had the unreasonable feeling that I had been talked into something by Curt Lang. But I hadn't been – responsibility for my actions has always been my own. I suppose it's the sensation that many travellers have: they've cut their veins and roots off from home, and it may be a long time before they can get the same necessary transfusion of familiar things elsewhere.

I was still enraptured with Layton's poems. I had two of his books with me, *The Cold Green Element* and *The Long Pea-Shooter*, to which was soon added *In the Midst of My Fever*. Irving's own talk and personality seemed to reflect directly from a poem like "It's All in the Manner," in which he says:

It's all in the manner of the done

> *Manner redeemeth everything:*
> *redeemeth*
> *man, sets him up among,*
> *over, the other worms, puts*
> *a crown on him, yes, size of a*
> > *mountain lake.*

That's a pretty attractive dosage of philosophy for a retarded thirty-five-year-old, and it's the quality that makes Layton so attractive to the young. It's the "Live, live, for tomorrow we die!" bit, and the thought behind it is absolutely damn well authentic. (Except that you can't mistake excess of anything for life itself.) For Layton, life was not over, it was in process and happening all the time.

"Manner redeemeth everything": but it damn well doesn't. You could cut somebody's throat with a swagger, ruin somebody's hope with a smiling word, alibiing yourself for both because of the gaiety and *insouciance* you employed in both murders. But when I saw the book and poem of the same name, *In the Midst of My Fever*, I was so jealous of that title that it made me feel hopeless, for now I would never be able to discover such a beautiful phrase myself. To the verbal hypnotism of the poems, Layton added his own charm, which seemed entirely natural and integral to the sort of person he was.

He drove us around Montreal in his bug-sized car, both he and I large men filling the bug to bursting, with Curt Lang squeezed right into the upholstery. At the Ritz Carlton pub we met Frank Scott to drink beer. Scott was feeling ebullient, since he'd just bought up cheaply all the copies of an early book of his from Ryerson Press, and was peddling them for the full price. Perhaps this was more profitable than publishing your own books.

And Louis Dudek, Layton's friend, who was teaching English at McGill, joined us for coffee in Murray's Restaurant. Dudek had a copy of my chapbook, *Pressed on Sand*, and was humorously taken aback to find me so elderly. "I thought you'd be twenty, and just beginning to shave," he said.

"How can Canadian poetry develop to greatness if its practitioners start at your age?"

Later Dudek pulled the poems in my book apart, one by one. Each of them had something wrong with it. His good humour was like that of a vivisectionist or a hangman, as he tore lines in half, exposing the attitudes they contained as second-hand imitations. "Why, man, Thomas Hardy said that fifty years ago" – pointing to a cherished passage.

I sat shamed and humiliated, tears in my eyes, but knowing I'd never stop writing and changing, no matter what Dudek or anyone else thought. Of course, Dudek's opinions were quite right, which didn't ease the rejection I felt, a male Cinderella kicked out of the party before the dancing started.

Despite this setback, when Layton drove us to the docks to board the steamer for Europe, my depression had vanished. The warmth and geniality that he radiated, and even Dudek's school-teacherish waspishness, seemed part of a rather marvellous Montreal scene. I knew I'd be back.

The next spring my wife, Eurithe, and I loaded up the red, '52 Chev and drove east from Vancouver. I'd been to Europe and back (with De Sade's *120 Days of Sodom*, Henry Miller's *Tropic of Capricorn*, and a book of dirty limericks under my shirt – passing customs left the book titles printed sweatily on my chest like a literary tattoo) and found a temporary job on returning with Grange Mattress. I'd bought an air pistol for my son in London, and during the entire eastward journey he sprayed lead pellets at motorists going in the other direction. We escaped arrest miraculously, but landed in Montreal quarreling violently, as usual.

We rented an apartment on Linton Avenue in the Côte des Neiges district of Montreal. My wife got a job at the CPR, as any good wife should in order to support her husband while he demonstrates his genius. I settled down to write plays for the CBC and poems for the breathless waiting world.

My wife and I went to see Irving Layton and Betty shortly after we got settled. The Laytons' glassed-in porch made a pleasant place for coffee and casual talk, with its condition of comfortable disarray and portraits of Irving on all the walls—including one of him umpiring a ball game at the Hertzeliah Secondary School where he taught. In the living room, occupying niches in the wall, were little shrines with candles burning inside to D.H. Lawrence and Bernard Shaw.

"Why, Irving," I said. "I thought you weren't religious."

"I am literarily religious, not theologically religious," he replied. "I make a distinction between the two. You, for instance, are neither one, and suffer from it in your writing." (Irving had the habit of making nearly everything he said unanswerable, his condition of pontificating being so normal that Betty said that they never needed a television set. Even if you had a point to make on the tip of your tongue, you couldn't get it said, for Irving would simply raise his voice one octave above the interruption and proceed.)

I changed the subject, but not very adroitly. Previously Irving had mentioned that I might be eligible for cleaning blackboards after Louis Dudek's class at McGill, expunging all references to iambic pentameter.

"Irving, what am I gonna do about money? Sure, my wife is working, but you can't expect even a willing horse to be willing forever." Eurithe's eyes flashed at the equine reference, but with an effort of supreme will she kept silent. "I've worked in factories for nearly six years, and I expect to be drawing unemployment insurance, but that won't last forever—"

Irving said nothing, and Betty kicked him on the ankle. "He's concentrating," she said. "You've seen yogas and other holy men? Irving hasn't got the character to be a real holy man, that's why he writes dirty poetry."

Irving kicked her back, but gently. "What about the National Film Board?" he said. "Their head office is here in Montreal, on Côte de Liesse. Anyone who writes the kind of poems you do should be able to write film scripts. And there are some lawns around here you could cut. . . ."

I was still fascinated by Irving Layton. He was actually a rather small man, somewhat run to fat, but who gave the impression of a much larger person. He had a presence, an almost visible aura that closed off things around him at times. Once, I saw him walking a downtown Montreal street reading a book, and even from a distance I knew it was Irving. He would have passed me without a word if I hadn't spoken; and after I did speak, he resumed reading with a concentration wholly uninterrupted. And his conversation was not spell-binding so much from the import of what he said, but rather from the power of his voice, the priest-like delivery and focal outpouring which turned the studio couch into an altar and his audience into a congregation.

At this time Irving's reputation was small. His books had mostly been published by himself. People who came into personal contact with Layton were hooked; his personality got them: and they bought his books. Irving Layton was then an archetypal example of the "underground poet," a writer who worked at his trade, dismissed by critics, ignored by newspaper reviewers and literary mags alike: a man who has since been transformed into an "establishment" figure, the *idée fixe* of a poet.

"Irving Layton sent me," said the man at my apartment door, shuffling his feet. "He said you wrote plays for the CBC and could give me some tips."

I told him to come in and we talked for four hours. It was a hot summer evening in Montreal in 1956, the first time I met Milton Acorn. He was from Prince Edward Island, thirty-four years old then, a man shaped like a wedge but without any taper. He seemed to bounce and shoulder his way through the air instead of walking in it. And yet sometimes he drifted over the pavement like the passage of a leaf. His voice was hesitant and slow–in the middle of a sentence he'd sometimes stop for several moments, then continue, already thinking of something else. Sometimes I could see the thought inside his mind that the words had not yet expressed, and I changed the subject for him before he finished the sentence.

Milton and I always argued, and much of my argument with him was because it was so entertainingly easy to disagree with the block-like certainties he expressed, the awesome absolutes of his political opinions. Of course, I had few hints to give him about writing plays, because I was a pretty mediocre playwright. But I felt terribly cocksure and positive of myself over a few things, such as the relativity of truth, which I attempted to use as a lever and a prod. Therefore, when Milton came up with one of his bedrock certainties, I was always the devil's advocate, even if I agreed with what he said: my how?, why?, and so what? providing a red flag for Milton's charging bull.

In the fall of 1956, Milton decided to sell his tools, he being a journeyman carpenter who had worked at the trade for years. I begged and pleaded with him not to take this step. "Milt," I said, "how can you make your living writing if a genius like me can't?"

Milton was silent a moment, and I thought he had gone to sleep. Then he said slowly and seriously, "Maybe it's you should buy the tools."

That stunned me for three full seconds. "At least keep the pawnbroker's tickets in case you get too many rejection slips," I said weakly.

During that winter Milt and I frequented the literary-party circuit in Montreal, mostly the Layton-Dudek axis, which had degenerated by that time into the cold formality of telephone calls and curt nods on the street. When Betty Layton had an exhibition of her paintings at a downtown gallery, Irving hurried her away when they met Dudek outside the building. Any friend of either Dudek or Layton was inevitably involved in the quarrel, and it was implicit that each felt his own friends were traitors if they fraternized with the other poet. Which produced feelings of discomfort in both myself and Acorn.

At Layton's house one night, Doug Kaye and I attacked Irving for his use of four-letter words. "Why try to shock people with 'fuck' and 'shit'?" Doug said, my own argument being much the same. Irving refuted us on every count, lifting his hand, raising his voice if one of us seemed about to interrupt, changing tone when he saw the expression in the back of our minds. Of course, the gist of his return argument was that four-letter words are a submerged and underground part of natural human speech, deleted by the nicey-nicey and eliminated by puritans, but still vibrant among the living words of undead human beings. (Amen!)

I now look back on that argument with amazement – not because I objected to four-letter words, but because when I read Layton's poems I see that there aren't any – or relatively few. In many of Layton's poems there is the feeling of licence, the sense of wickedness and forbidden things for some people, at least – the things that made Henry Miller attractive but that are now fairly familiar. Irving was quite right when he declared that language was unnatural and stilted when polite circles avoided such words. But the world has now passed beyond such trivialities, perhaps to other trivialities in turn.

There were some good parties that winter, at Louis Dudek's house, at Layton's, and also those in the Purdy apartment when my friends, Henry Ballon, Doug Kaye, and I, along with whatever guests were there, tried desperately to consume all the home-made beer that we had in stock. The new batch was almost always ready, and we needed empty bottles. Beer was practically foaming out of our ears, and mineral water bottles of it were jammed into every closet, with scarcely room for clothes. However, bootlegging was considered only as a last resort, and it was a matter of pride that we drank all we could produce: the kind of pride that goeth before a you-know-what.

One party remains in my mind as a kind of super-party, with an impenetrable haze surrounding the location – as well as my own movements when it ended. (The suspect entered a movie house, sat quietly for half an hour, when the feature started he left and committed a dastardly murder. His actual movements cannot be traced.) At one point during the evening I remember lying on the floor, arm-wrestling with Layton, with the praying mantis form of Louis Dudek looming over us for referee. "And these are supposed to be sensitive poets!" he intoned superciliously. Now why the hell shouldn't sensitive poets arm-wrestle?

When spring came to Montreal in 1957 it was an anticlimax, for everyone had been expecting it for years. That summer Eurithe and I were at Roblin Lake, building an A-frame.

The time between 1957 and 1959 was the low period of my life so far. Every morning and afternoon, if I wasn't working at some odd job elsewhere, I sat down at the typewriter to hammer out plays for the CBC. I plotted them in my head and on paper, reading the newspapers for topical hints of new ones, consulting the Belleville library for references. But whatever writing touch I might have possessed before was now lost: whatever I wrote met with swift rejection. The neighbours were pitying my wife in these days – she told me later – because she had married such a bum who wouldn't work.

It's quite likely that I had some sort of mental block about actually accepting a permanent job in Toronto or Montreal. My efforts in that direction appeared to me as sometimes half-hearted, and I was easily discouraged by my own moods of black depression. If I had found a decent-paying job, this would have meant complete defeat in a writing sense – or so I told myself gloomily. Here I was, nearly forty years old, knowing nothing but nothing, except writing: and that was problematical. How sad it all was!

By the summer of 1959 money was entirely lacking. My wife and I arranged to move back to Montreal to stay with Henry and Annette Ballon until we found jobs. Eurithe was taken on by a pharmaceutical firm as a secretary, and I went to work for Johnston's Mattress Company on St. Germain in Montreal East. Johnston's was a United Nations sort of factory, with dark Sicilians and Greeks working next to French-

Canadians and Jews. I hadn't worked in four years, and my forty-year-old muscles were in terrible shape.

Pierre, the upholsterer, didn't like Jews: he thought that they were the root of all the world's evil. When I learned about this from Pierre, something perverse in myself caused me to drop little clues to him that I was Jewish, having "passed" in Gentile society as a white negro might into white society. For a week I was able to maintain this fiction, until Pierre began to question me closely about the Jewish religion. I was completely ignorant of the Talmud Torah or whatever the book is, since Henry and Annette, Irving Layton, and all the other Jewish people I knew then didn't practise their religion.

For whatever reason – and it was probably because of the Montreal Jewish areas in which we happened to live – our circle of friends and acquaintances was almost entirely Jewish. As far as I'm concerned, they are the liveliest and most intellectually alert people I know. By comparison, some people of Anglo-Saxon descent seem stodgy and half-asleep. Pierre, the journeyman upholsterer at Johnston's, must have agreed, for he thought that the world's banks were controlled by an international cabal of Jewish financiers.

Among the first things I did on my return to Montreal was to visit Irving Layton. The old charisma he exerted over me still worked: not quite a hex, but more than a fascination. Irving now lived on a street off Côte des Neiges, not far from our newly rented apartment on Maplewood. He had also acquired a new wife, Aviva (the name means springtime), from Australia. I didn't know why Irving and Betty broke up, and it was none of my business. But Aviva was certainly one of the nicer things that happened to Irving: and thinking of Betty before Aviva, he had a talent for attracting women who, if not goddesses, were at least nereides. Irving himself was decidedly mortal.

On the wall beside the kitchen table the dust jacket of *A Red Carpet for the Sun* – soon to be published by McClelland & Stewart – was scotchtaped. Aviva hovered and fluttered about like a nervous butterfly. Irving's mother had died not long before, and he read me the inevitable poem about it and the "inescapable lousiness of growing old." Irving explained all the symbolic O's, the black holes and circles in the poem, explained them like the professor he had recently become at Sir George Williams University. But like a kind of unlettered simpleton, I thought the poem beautiful regardless of levels of meaning placed inside it, as if it were a fifty-storey condominium waiting for critical ghosts to begin the haunting.

Layton had the habit of reading his poems as if he were in the presence of the holy sepulchre, and a large fragment of the true cross had lodged in his mouth. One faced this atmosphere whether the poems he read were among his more trivial efforts or best, although most of the time they were his best. And he praised himself in such glowing terms that the listener was unable to decide whether to kneel in prayer, or to make obeissance in the oriental manner by knocking his forehead on the floor, or to join the eulogy with words that could not possibly reach the heights of self-praise that Layton's own achieved.

Shortly after assuming the professorship at Sir George Williams, Irving didn't merely have followers hanging on his words raptly—he had disciples. But the personal fascination that Layton exerted over me had subsided to only a strong liking by about 1961. I came back to Montreal from the west coast in that year, arranging to meet Layton in a downtown pub. Both of us had written new poems, he a sonnet and I a verse I've completely forgotten now. Layton tore this poem of mine apart with much more venom than Dudek had the earlier poem, and (I thought) with unfairness; so I defended it vigorously. In turn, Layton read his own sonnet, and declared it would out-live Shakespeare. I contested that opinion of what I thought was a less-than-ordinary poem, some slight heat being generated in the discussion.

We were both right and both wrong. To get into such an argument in the first place is a measure of the passion that both of us felt for poetry. But I have always been unable to remain angry with Layton. I think he is childish and trivial, egocentric and overbearing, boastful and dangerously harmful to others influenced by him – but he remains in my mind as close to a great poet as any I know of who is still living.

Louis Dudek was about as different a person from Layton as is possible to conceive. In conversation he is tentative much of the time, although when talking about Pound and W.C. Williams and their theories about ordinary speech in prosody, he became as magisterial and priest-like as most find it convenient to be when talking down to lesser beings. But to me Dudek's personal charm and curious detachment caused me to seek him out as if I were one of Layton's own shadowy acolytes. Dudek was theoretic and tentative, as opposed to Layton's certainty: the latter quality generally has a tub-thumping attraction for the listener.

In Montreal, during my Johnston Mattress tenure, Louis Dudek was running a poetry magazine called *Delta*. It was entirely a one-man show – although I think Ron Everson may have helped, and I assisted in the mailing operations at intervals. There were parties at Dudek's house on winter Saturdays that surpassed any previously. I suppose you'd call some of them "intellectual," in a non-denigrating sense. One evening novelist Hugh MacLennan held forth for several hours on historical necessity and the predictability of events in relation to a classical education. Layton never appeared at these parties.

My favourite image of Dudek comes from a trip we made together, driving to Stanley House in the Maritimes from Montreal with Louis and Mike Gnarowski. Dudek sat in the front seat, wearing a beret and horn-rimmed glasses, looking somewhat like a giant mosquito: he was six feet two and weighed only 160 pounds.

E. J. Pratt had just died, and the three of us composed a dirge for his death, to the tune of "The Bonnie Earl of Moray." Dudek played the Scottish tune over and over on his mouth organ, while Gnarowski and I sang the elegy for Pratt in accompaniment. At gas stations Louis told the attendants that I was the idiot son of a Texas oil millionaire, and he was my paid guardian. I had to be watched closely because I might wander off into the bush and damage myself. Finding out about this later endeared Louis to me.

When I returned to Montreal that fall of 1959, Milton Acorn had moved from St. Antoine to Sanguinet Street. When I visited him he was trying to write science-fiction for a living, his floor knee-deep in papers and the general overwhelming rubble of a man without a woman. One of his stories was a beautiful fairy tale, "The Red and Green Pony," which impressed the hell out of me. And there was a letter just arrived from Whit Burnett of *Story* magazine, expressing interest in Milton's fiction. And, snobbishly, I began to wonder if an ex-carpenter had ever received the Nobel Prize.

That was perhaps the high point of Milton's literary exuberance, when he thought he had it made if only he could keep going, if only he didn't starve to death first, if only – but, sadly, the "if onlys" prevailed. Milton would run out of money, then come to stay with my wife and me at our apartment on Maplewood. I was working by this time, and Milton, sleeping on a spare mattress on the floor and eating enormously, was little burden except for the dinner dishes.

We continued to argue about everything. I'm not sure how this was possible between two people who remained friends, but I ascribe it to his slow good nature and refusal to allow anything to shake his faith in the essential nobility of man and the Communist Manifesto. By contrast, I had a personal necessity to question everything generally regarded as universal law – and I mean everything.

Sometimes Milton took low and underhanded advantages in our anything-goes "discussions": he would read all my books for ammunition, then fire the arguments back at me faster than I could read my own books. Once he read a four-volume set of Freud's essays (free gift from a book club) from cover to cover before I even opened it, and had such a fund of psychological information as to confound me completely when I came home from work tired as hell after the eight-hour grind. But after a nap, I read frantically to catch up on Freud and thus protect myself in such unfair semantic clinches.

Milton and I started our little magazine, *Moment*, in the fall of 1959. He had found a mimeograph machine somewhere–I think he "borrowed" it from the Communist party– and we ran off each issue on the floor of the Purdy apartment. The reasons for *Moment* were both egotistic (we wanted to publish our own poems, although I denied this to Milt) and altruistic (we wanted to publish good poems by other people). And I wrote letters to anyone who I thought might have poems worth publishing, including Phyllis Gotlieb, Ralph Gustafson, and several others. We were both rather proud of publishing Wade Hemsworth's "Black Flies of North Ontario," thus proving an eclecticism that did not exclude our own poems.

In the early spring of 1960, when I quit my job at Johnston's mattress factory, feeling physically dog-tired and worn-out, Milton came with me when I returned to the house at Roblin Lake. Heavy snow was still on the ground and thick ice covered the lake. Stovewood sawed from railway ties and lumber was used up, but a supply of heavy boards was still available. Milton and I cut wood with a handsaw, trying to keep warm, and telling ourselves that the exercise was good for us. It wasn't. Anyone who has ever cut stovewood with a handsaw would agree. We damn near killed ourselves in an endurance contest with the weather and our old Quebec heater in the living room.

In April two boxcar loads of ties and scrap lumber were given to me by the CPR simply for hauling them away. I rented a truck, and Milton and I worked several days loading and unloading, hauling potential stovewood to Roblin Lake. After that, we tinkered at the house and wrote poems.

A literary conference took place in Kingston that spring. I urged Milton to go, although he was pretty backward about going. He hitchhiked to Kingston and was gone for two days. When he came back, I found out he'd been too shy to speak to anyone at the conference, and had watched the people going in and out of the auditorium, feeling left out of everything. A park bench near the university had supplied him with sleeping quarters for those two nights, and in April it was still cold. I laughed at Milton for that, but it wasn't actually very humorous. He was still the outsider, in all ways.

You couldn't spend two minutes in his company without knowing that he's a deep-dyed red Marxist, his complexion being no accident. Politics and humanism pervade his conversation and many of his poems. And while there have been excellent Marxist poets in the world – such as Bertolt Brecht, Mayakovsky, Neruda, – there had been none in Canada of more than minor ability – not until Acorn came along. And yet, it is a paradox that he has disagreed with, fought, quarreled, and resigned in holy rage from any and every socialist organization he ever worked for, including the Chinese Trotskyites, and is a member in good standing of none. If you deduce from this that Acorn is a red-necked maverick with tender corns, both in politics and poetry, then you are right.

Once Acorn and I visited Leonard Cohen in the latter's apartment in Montreal. If ever two men were exact antitheses of each other, they were Cohen and Acorn; the first giving the impression of elegant aristocracy, wearing a dressing gown to putter around the kitchen in while preparing coffee. Cohen seemed to me on that morning to be entirely self-aware, completely adjusted and comfortable in his surroundings. So much so that he moved within a slight but perceptible aura of decadence – decadence not in the form of decline, but of standing aside in weariness, having been through life before and found it slightly boring. One gets this same feeling in some of his poems, excellent as they are. Even in "Suzanne," perhaps the best folksong lyric of its kind ever written in this country, there is an exotic and fateful sense of being on another level of consciousness than the mundane world of work and wages. Of course, I am sure Cohen knows this well, for he strives toward another level of being, a breakthrough into a more meaningful existence.

But on that morning the languid and rather overcultured

Jewish aristocrat was foremost. By contrast, Acorn: the red fire hydrant in blue denims. One would almost think that one or the other of the two men had staged this meeting in order to feel more strongly and deeply the things that they already were. Acorn: slow in his impulsiveness, stutteringly inarticulate, the lava bed of his personality covered with shyness and the awkward aplomb of those who are self-righteously right, recently escaped from the noble servitude of labour, completely alien in that apartment of Cohen's, whose furnishings and decor were the result of a cultivated mind and personality.

After we drank espresso coffee the conversation got around to politics, a topic quite inevitable when Acorn is involved. And Cohen said, "Milton, if communism is ever outlawed in Canada, and the Mounties round up all dangerous subversives, you'd be among the first arrested."

Of course, Cohen was exactly right. On the other hand, if an equivalent of the French Revolution ever occurred in Canada, Leonard Cohen would also stand out like an aristocratic sore thumb.

But I am making this cultured quality in Cohen sound like something shameful, something to be despised by all members of the proletariat in good standing. This is an entirely wrong impression. If Cohen ever did fit my description, he has altered since.

Acorn is a black-and-white man. What human being would not publicly protest that he was on the side of good and against evil? Or that he stood for life as opposed to death? But such blindness is Acorn's strength: whereas Cohen's idealism lies largely in the knowledge of human evil and guilt, which also resides in himself, and admits to both. And while we might immediately say that we prefer Cohen's brand of idealism, only abstracted from both these writers' poems could this be true.

In 1962 Acorn married Gwen MacEwen in Toronto, with me handing him the ring at City Hall. The couple lived on Toronto Island that winter, but the marriage didn't last. In 1963 Acorn went to Vancouver, continuing to write poems, aided now by a pension that came as a result of his war experiences.

Milton Acorn has been involved in some odd events in his lifetime, a few of them publishable, the others not. But the testimonial dinner for him in 1970 at Grossman's Tavern, Toronto, was one of the strangest. That evening still remains distorted and surrealistic in my memory.

Acorn sat at Grossman's head table, with Layton, Eli Mandel, and other friends beside him. A silver medal, dangling from his neck on a purple ribbon, bore the words, "Milton Acorn, The People's Poet." In front of the ceremonial table swirled the kind of people you occasionally see at Grossman's – beer-drinkers and bums, dead beats and free loaders, even a few genuine workers.

The evening wore on, with newspaper reporters reporting and CBC men, wearing that questing look of basset hounds, searching for someone who knew more than they did. Layton made a speech, Mandel made a speech, and so did Acorn. Acorn displayed his medal, there was applause and beer. By about ten o'clock Grossman's was so jammed that the waiters had to hold their beer trays high above their heads. The tavern seemed full of swaying yellow suns. I was escorting a girl through the dense human crush to the lady's john when a guy hove in sight from the port side and said, "Fuck off!" I addressed him mildly, saying, "Do I know you?" Again he repeated the same instructions, of dubious benefit to myself, and I'm afraid he had something of a one-track mind. By this time a slight suspicion entered my mind that the man had no very friendly intentions, so I pushed him vigorously into the laps of some beer-drinkers. They pushed him back, setting the stage for open hostilities. Then the waiters spotted him, and – having mistaken me for Mayor Dennison because they'd seen me swallow a microphone earlier, and feeling some regard for the dignity of high municipal office – they threw the jerk out.

The party at Grossman's was half farce and half solemn

event. In my mind the two were difficult to separate. Scores of friends paying tribute to Acorn: CBC and newspaper reporters; the drunk with the two-word soundtrack—and Milton himself, progressing through the room a little swacked, and I think very happy about being "The People's Poet," his medal dangling on a purple ribbon, soon to be stained with soup. Perhaps that was the strangest part of all—the proud medal.

There are human differences I'll never fully understand; but Acorn's poems transcended such differences and made even Grossman's Tavern only a room full of people. I recalled his lines in a poem: "I play my mauled rainbeaten pack plus near three billion others, all to win." That night at Grossman's, Acorn won.

Bon Jour?

About ten years ago my wife and I were driving through Quebec, along the St. Lawrence River's south shore. We stopped at little villages, emitting oohs and ahs at the architecture of houses and churches, stopping when it felt comfortable to stop. We looked at the home craftsmanship in museums and local displays; crossed a river by ferry, connecting with a cable to the other shore; we met a cordial priest, who gave us a conducted tour of his old church, a place in which the whole interior felt touched and used by generations of people.

At one point we found ourselves driving over flat countryside, and had decided by then that we'd better speed up a little in order to reach our destination in the Maritimes before laziness overcame us entirely. Then another car appeared ahead of us, with Quebec license plates. It drove between 15 and 20 miles per hour, and stayed directly in the road centre. My wife was patient for perhaps a quarter of an hour, then she beeped the horn. The car ahead stopped immediately, in the road's centre, and my wife braked our car. We looked at each other. Omigawd, I thought, and we both thought: the guy has seen our Ontario license plates in the rear view mirror, and now some racial unpleasantness is about to happen.

I got out of the car, walked around to the driver's side, got behind the wheel, and gunned it around the Quebec car, narrowly avoiding the ditch. The good feeling we had about being there was destroyed. And I've sometimes wondered since if I would have taken the same evasive action if the same incident had occurred in English-speaking Canada. It's doubtful; I am not notably meek in such situations.

But it's entirely unfair to base an opinion of Quebec on such an incident. I lived in Montreal a few years ago. Frank Scott, poet and ex-professor of law at McGill, provided a kind of meeting place for French and English. He was and still is the catalyst, enabling the two races to join in an atmosphere of cordiality and liking. Among others, I met Jean Palardy, connoisseur and author of books on Quebec furniture, and Gilles Hennault, the poet, at Scott's place. And they were generous enough to speak English since my high-school French is almost non-existent.

By any standards I can think of, the Quebec Premier, Réne Lévesque, is a man of good will. I don't happen to agree with his politics of Quebec separation, but no one could possibly deny that Lévesque is the most natural person and human politician it's possible to meet, whether on television or anywhere else. I met him six years ago in Montreal, when *Maclean's* magazine wanted me to write an article about him. The meeting has coloured all my thoughts about Quebec ever since.

Arriving at Parti Québécois headquarters, I'm a little early for my appointment at 2:00 PM, and walk around the Avenue Christophe Colomb area. It's commonplace and working-class, bakeries, garages, small apartment blocks, the CN railway tracks nearby—so humdrum ordinary you think nothing could ever happen here but babies. In six years I don't suppose it's changed much.

At the bright blue PQ building, with a fleur-de-lis flag waving, cam-

paign workers dash around bearing dispatches and café au lait. A girl brings me a chair: Lévesque is late. Like a brisk small general he appears forty minutes later, carrying a briefcase, shakes my hand and says, "I'm sorry I kept you waiting. Be with you in five minutes."

Upstairs in his office Lévesque fiddles with papers, and nearly disappears behind a huge desk. I feel silly. I mean, me and twenty questions for a guy who's heard them all before. Not awe-struck—nobody could possibly feel that way with Lévesque. Hair brushed sideways from vanity across his bald head, puffing his millionth cigarette, tanned and healthy looking, not sallow and pale as on television. The exact opposite of bearded heroic Fidel Castro leading his rebels down a dirt road in Cuba's Oriente Province. And yet Lévesque is definitely a rebel, he says so himself.

But if he's heard all my twenty questions before, I've heard all his own answers before—on television and in the newspapers. So what's the point of this interview? I guess it has to be impressionistic, its relevance tied to what I think of Lévesque personally. As well, the answer he gave to just one question of mine: "What do you think is your particular strength, the quality that makes you leader of the PQ? I mean, is it personality, vote-getting, decision-making or what?"

Lévesque says, "I am one of the most typical Québécois. That's my strength. When I feel something the people will be close behind. In Quebec, I represent the mainstream of change, the time that is nearly upon us."

"The time that is nearly upon us" has arrived. Six years after that interview René Lévesque is Premier of his province. Within the next few months there will undoubtedly be a referendum in Quebec, at a time when Lévesque is reasonably certain that his people will vote for separation from the rest of Canada. The murder of Pierre Laporte by shadowy terrorists is long past; his killers are sweating out their exile in Cuba. And at this precise moment, Lévesque and his *confrères* are at the crest of an emotional high that would shame every LSD and speed addict in the world. Moses leads the Children of Israel out of Egypt; Simon Bolivar rides again; Leonidas is shaking his rusty sword at the Persians and cussing in joual, *"Maudit Anglais,"* or something; Taras Shevchenko and Vladimir Lenin are tall in the saddle; the

Boston tea-party is now equalization payments and the integrity of the French language in Quebec air-space. (I do think the part about air-space is a bit of a come-down.)

But get back to that statement of Lévesque's, that he is one of the most typical of the Québécois. Does everyone feel as he does, that separation is the only answer? The polls say no, only about 25 per cent feel that way. But the opinion polls aren't all-seeing and all-knowing. Time is actually on the side of the *Séparatistes*. And this latter twentieth century is a historic and fortunate time for the freedom-seekers, the age favours them: Vietnamese gutting invading Americans in their pestilent jungles; Basques in a small corner of Spain shrieking Freedom; Welsh and Scots in Britain murmuring discontentedly; African nations throwing off the shackles of their colonialist masters, etc., etc. And notice the terminology that seems impossible to escape: "freedom" (that old catchword), "throwing off the shackles," and so on.

What much of all this boils down to is an end-product of the old fierce blood-letting wars between England and France. When British Wolfe knocked off French Montcalm at Quebec in 1759, he set up a train of events the weak-chinned general could never possibly have anticipated. The defeated French have disliked and sometimes hated their conquerors ever since. Never mind all the polite talk from Ottawa and elsewhere, never mind the Quebec Prime Ministers like Wilfrid Laurier, Louis St. Laurent and now Pierre Trudeau. To many Québécois, these men of their own race were and are traitors and sell-outs. Never mind equalization payments. Pay no attention to any good that has come to Quebec as a result of being part of this loose (very loose) federation of Canadian provinces. Ignore goodwill, if you like, since it's apparently quite irrelevant in 1977. There's very little of it around.

In certain important respects, Quebec is quite right in disliking the English. (Of course we are no longer English, and they are no longer French.) As any self-respecting eighteenth century conqueror might be expected to do, the English took over all or most commercial, financial and military aspects of the new territory. Why not? It was the habit and tradition then to loot a conquered country. (It's still the custom, although methods used vary from one conqueror to another.) And if anyone doubts that this happened, take a fast look at the stately homes of Westmount in their stone splendour on the slopes of Mount Royal.

After 1759, the English dominated; then English Canadians took over that job; and now, rather ambiguously, it's Canadians. What many Québécois have lost sight of is the USA, omnipresent in both Quebec language and industry. Americans appear to escape Québécois dislike, despite their being originally English; the mouse does not dislike the elephant, but hates the sight of what looks like a cat.

What I'm saying is: if I'd been born in Quebec, then very likely I'd be a minor henchman or small plotter, too unimportant to be closer than six ranks away from Lévesque. Yes, a *Séparatiste*. Like that guy who stopped his car at the dead centre of the road in Quebec hinterlands ten years ago, hating the Ontario Anglais, hating me.

No Québécois fears that he personally will lose his language; he fears his children will. And when, a hundred years from now, the continent is completely anglicised, he fears that the people who lived in 1977, his people, will appear as oddities, not completely real, an aberration that history has corrected for the greater good of the human whole. At which date, Québécois children will not know their fathers, be ignorant of the struggles at Ville Marie on the island of Montreal, unaware of Adam Dollard and Madeleine de Verchères, the great French drum-roll of history and ma- and pa-ternity (oblivious to their father Pierre and mother Marie).

The children will not know, or knowing think it irrelevant and unimportant. And that fear is the fear we all have: that when we die and our bones rot, our unimportant lives forgotten, even our descendants will harbour no trace in themselves of what we were. The ongoing wave of time will not carry us with it: we will be what we are in our most spiritually depressed moments – nothing. (And of course, this passion for personal survival is a salient characteristic of the entire human race.) We would like to think that if we were able to send our misty astral self back after a thousand years, to explore the place in which we were born – we would like to believe that even after the lapse of millennia of time and distance, a child could be heard to whisper father and mother, or *mère* and *père*.

Is that gushy and sentimental? I hope not. And the words we speak, somehow only that, the Word, the thing we entered and which entered us, is all that can possibly survive of dying and being born and rising again as the grass springs green and the flesh is grass.

Reach back to 1960. In that year I worked for a mattress factory in Montreal East called Johnston's. Having spent some five years in Vancouver learning to operate the various machines used in the manufacture of mattresses (tape-edge, tufting, filler and roll-edge), it was inevitable that they would give me a job of which I was completely ignorant, making boxsprings. It was fated by the gods at Johnston's that I learn how to make boxsprings; and Hymie Sloan was the prophet of those gods.

If ever there was a dog's breakfast of nationalities in one place, it was Johnston's on St. Germain. It included Guiseppe from somewhere around Naples, fat little Tony from Sicily who once tried to put a hex on me (and thought he'd succeeded when I came to work with a black eye one Monday), assorted Québécois, including Pierre (who thought Jewish bankers controlled the world), and pale Thérèse in the cutting room, delicate Thérèse who was more beautiful than a straight seam. Top dog of this mongrel assemblage was Hymie Sloan, whose wisdom consisted of being Jewish, and thus in Pierre's mind kin to all the bankers who manipulate and control our spinning globe. Hymie was also foreman. The factory owners were English-speaking, but I never did find out if they were American, English or possibly even Canadian.

The language spoken in that factory was whatever you happened to be able to mumble with your mouth full of tacks, or remembered as your birthright; i.e., it was anything. Pierre, a journeyman upholsterer, worked next to me, and spoke perfect French and English, giving me valuable hints on boxspring making in English between the tacks in his mouth, and I suspect cussing me in French for my slow-learning abilities.

Listening to Pierre talk about Jews controlling the financial world, I had a bright idea. At least it seemed bright at the time. I began to let slip tell-tale Jewish phrases, dropping them into the conversation as if by accident, then covering up by hurrying the conversation onto another subject. (I didn't know very many Jewish words at first, and had to ask Leslie Mayer and Henry Ballon for more ammunition while we were making home-made beer in my apartment—but that's another story.) Pierre forced me to admit eventually that lox, bagel and kosher fodder were my native diet, in short, that I was Jewish. His impression was that previously I had masqueraded as non-Jewish. Later, when he cornered me with questions about the Talmud Torah and tough theologic conundrums, my imposture fell apart. But always after this episode, Pierre could never be absolutely sure that I wasn't an elderly child of Israel; and sometimes I caught him looking at me with wild surmise. It's the first time I was ever mistaken for a Jewish banker.

Anyway—downstairs in the foreign territory of French and Italian was Jacques. And Jacques could be called, on some very elemental level, the Bull of the Shop. He weighed only about 175 pounds compared to my 200, but was some fifteen years younger and in top physical shape. Jacques was very proud of his feats of physical strength, moving through the factory like a big cat with the hot-foot, everyone much aware that he was boss.

Eventually it came to the ears of the Bull of the Shop that a large Anglo newcomer on the floor above had delusions of physical grandeur. Jungle tom-toms wove their ominous music among the machines; grape vines whispered that denouement was inevitable. Tony, Pierre and Hymie Sloan knew it; and maybe even my beautiful Thérèse, whose eyes were dark pools in the moon-pallor of her face–maybe even she knew it. And they licked their lips in antcipation.

It started with a grin–from Jacques standing beside my work table. I knew what that grin meant. I grinned back; he knew what I meant. But since Jacques knew only a word or two of English and ditto me of French, it was somewhat like a jungle dialogue of "Me Tarzan, you Jane."

Arm-wrestling was the opening of hostilities. I insisted on using my left arm, my trusty left arm that had previously defeated pretenders to my non-existent title when I was in the RCAF years before. Besides, my right arm was lame, or so I conveyed to Jacques in pantomime. As things turned out, I won so quickly it was no contest, and discontent furrowed the manly brow of the Bull of the Shop. His prestige in the factory descended to the point where even little Tony dared to grin; and Thérèse, whom he loved with dumb passion, ignored him.

Battle was joined once more during noon-hour. Bull of the Shop and Anglo wrestled between the machines, kicking up clouds of dust and choking interested spectators. Jacques was very strong, his legs and arms toughened by toil. And Thérèse watched him admiringly in the front-row seats. We sweated, we rolled on the dusty wooden floor, first one and then the other having an advantage. But I knew he was too young and strong for me; if the contest continued for more than six rounds nothing could save me but the referee–and we didn't have one.

Lunging and charging each other, we suddenly found ourselves in the men's john, and simultaneously had the idea of trying to duck the other in the toilet. Summoning reserves of endurance from a younger existence I wrestled the Bull to a standstill, and that was what it was, a standstill. We clasped each other unlovingly and sweatily above the porcelain bowl. Then one of us started to laugh. I don't remember which it was, but then we both laughed. We pointed to each other, grinning, as if to say, "Look at you, what a silly damn fool I am and we are." Then I became conscious of a strong odour–and it wasn't Chanel #5.

The battle was declared a draw. After that Jacques and I became, if not cordial, rather more wary of each other. I didn't intend to take another chance on getting my neck broken in that bastard's hands; and perhaps he wasn't quite so eager to break it. His French and my English didn't mingle, but our sweat did. Thérèse again gazed on him, her moon-pallor tinged with attractive pink deriving from her innermost thoughts. And while I do not recommend the confrontation of elephant bulls as an aid to *détente* between French and English, it worked for Jacques and me. When I quit the factory a few months later Hymie Sloan shook hands; so did Pierre. Jacques, my necessary antagonist, also shook hands, and grinned slyly. (I think he knew he had me if our Roman games had continued). I don't know if we were friends, but we sure as hell weren't enemies.

It's hard to say whether such incidents have any real meaning; but in the wake of the Parti Québécois victory in Quebec, one re-examines them wondering what it is they signify. One thing I am sure of, and that is that the attitudes of English-speaking Canada towards Quebec have changed greatly. Oh, of course there are still some elements everywhere in Canada that say of the Québécois: "Let them go if they want to go so badly. They're more trouble than they're worth." At a time when simple justice is now possible for them, in the matter of language and economics, it seems they no longer want to be part of the larger federal union inside Canada.

And that is tragic to me, tragic that even after two hundred years our two races cannot settle their differences amicably. After two hundred years, race hatred is still strong; and that's what it is, race hatred. Of course they are somewhat paranoid, an easy thing to understand, isolated on their small Francophone island in a sea of English. The age-old phony catchwords of "freedom" and "masters in our own house" will probably destroy all bridges to the mainland. And make no mistake, everything outside Quebec is the mainland of this North American continent: no matter what emotional high Lévesque and his dedicated men are riding, isolation is neither attractive nor possible. Freedom, they say, and freedom they will have, come hell or heaven; and it will not be heaven. That desired haven is not available to any of us, no matter what our nationality may be.

Being alive in the twentieth century, it's never possible to get far away from such things as unemployment, strikes, economic exploitation, separatism, murder, corruption in high places, and so on. These are the constants of all our lives. But there are a few other worthwhile things besides in human existence: like trying to find purpose and meaning in your own day-to-day living, or exploring someone else's personality in relation to your own. And a country, any country, ought to be a kind of cocoon wrapped around each of us that permits such exploration, allows us to discover our own value, our own meaning as it relates to other people.

That is idealistic, and we have no time for it, because of our lives' outer turmoil. Strikes, political quarrels and constitutional squabbles must be settled first, to provide at least a personal clearing in the human jungle. But they are never settled, and there is never time. The sense of well-being when the sun shines is brief, the fixed instant of rapport with another person passes, and it seems we have imagined the memory.

And after a hundred years, if a Quebec car moving at 15 miles per hour over the green countryside stops, blocking passage of an Ontario car, what then? Will the drivers get out of their cars and shake hands? Of course not. But perhaps, hopefully, one might say, "Bon Jour"?

"Good morning," – then.

Aklavik on the Mackenzie River

They came over the land bridge connecting Asia with Alaska, those first men in the Western Hemisphere. The date was between 20,000 and 30,000 years ago. They were short and heavily built people with thick black hair, brown faces, and slightly slanted eyes. They were hunters, dressed in the skins of animals they hunted. Their weapons were stone-tipped spears. All this was long before Homer, before the dynasties of Egypt, before Sumer and the Land of the Two Rivers, and, of course, long before our Christian Bible was written.

At that time the glaciers that had covered Canada and parts of the northeastern United States during the last ice age were melting. They melted first along river valleys, which turned into great misty, fog-haunted corridors between receding walls of ice. One of these river-valley corridors is known today as the Mackenzie River in the Northwest Territories.

The hunters roamed south along melting corridors of ice,

pursuing animals for food and clothing. They died eventually, as all people do, and their children came after them in the long stammering repetition of humanity everywhere. The animals they hunted were principally caribou, bear, and mammoth – the latter long since extinct in North America. Camps of some of those early men have been discovered recently. They are the ghostly forbears of modern Indians and Eskimos.

"Coffee, sir?" the Pacific Western Airlines stewardess wants to know. She is black-haired and shapely, almost distracting me from my thoughts about those early people. I'm flying north from Edmonton to read poems at libraries of settlements in the Northwest Territories. I decline coffee politely and ask for beer. There is none.

Under me and under the big aeroplane is the Mackenzie River, concealed at this moment by cloud cover. The Mackenzie River drainage system is the biggest in Canada. It rises in the Rocky Mountains with the name of Athabaska, which flows east and then north to its namesake lake. The Slave River flows north from Lake Athabaska to empty into Great Slave Lake; and forty miles from Hay River on this lake, the true Mackenzie begins its thousand-mile journey north to the Beaufort Sea.

At 7:15 PM on May 23, we land at Inuvik Airport. Dick Hill, the quiet-mannered director of Inuvik Research Laboratories, drives me to town over a dirt road. High plumes of dust trail behind every car. I register at the Eskimo Inn, which has seventy-nine rooms and colour TV via satellite. Taxis outside are coated with half-inch-thick layers of dust. Taxis and colour TV! Can this be the Arctic of fierce husky dogs and bearded veterans of the north?

The temperature is about 40°F; population is about 5000 people, living and working in buildings resting on piles to make their uneasy peace with the permafrost, which under us is a thousand-foot-thick ice animal crouching. After falling asleep around 11 PM, I awake briefly at four to find that the day still hasn't stopped or night begun. It is comforting to find that my childhood myths about the land of the midnight sun and its red-mouthed slavering polar bears were not entirely imaginary.

On Saturday, May 24, the sun shining and the air outside is comfortable for me clad in tweed jacket and sweater. The big question now is how to get to Aklavik, "place of the barren ground grizzly bear," thirty-five miles across the Mackenzie delta. There are no roads. On weekdays, there are commercial flights for paying passengers. But it's Saturday, so I hope to share a charter with someone else.

Aklavik is still a mythic place for me, the big reason why I wanted so badly to come to the western Arctic. Built on sand and sediment thirty feet above the Mackenzie's Peel Channel, threatened by floods every spring (and right now it's spring), inhabited by picturesque trappers and hunters, old codgers breathing history and fire from their own homebrew (I read that somewhere), its existence began in 1915. When the federal government in its wisdom decided in 1954 that Aklavik was unfortunately situated, the town seemed doomed. The new modern Arctic settlement of Inuvik ("the place of man") began to rise on wooden piles in that year, complete with government buildings and schools, fresh water and sewage alike contained in above-ground metal utilidors. The native Indians and Eskimos were supposed to throng to the the new town with cries of ecstasy, and some of them did. But it turned out they had to live in the old workers' construction shacks, whereas white workers moved into the newly built houses. Many natives thought they were better off in Aklavik, closer to their traplines, less dependent on white men, and perhaps also closer to their own kind of reality.

So Aklavik refused to lie down and die. Hemmed in by marshes and water, plagued with erosion and haunted by periodic river flooding, it was still a settlement that grew up naturally because of hunting, fishing, and trapping in the delta. There was nothing phony or artificial about it – quite the opposite of the oil-exploration and government town deliberately created at Inuvik; created scientifically and a little cold-bloodedly, a hovering outpost of southern man near the Arctic Sea. Aklavik's character is slightly raffish, a little off-colour–perhaps not quite so respectable. But it's much closer to my own romantic idea of the north, of Eskimos living comfortably amid ice and snow, of arctic explorers and dog teams galloping across the tundra. The Canadian arctic has changed greatly, and no longer are the old and admittedly romantic conceptions possible. Just the same, I cling to them; I like the idea of a town like Aklavik, rejecting the outside world–but, significantly, not its electricity and septic tanks.

I flew to Aklavik on Sunday in a Cessna 180. These tiny aeroplanes resemble an exceptionally large mosquito that climbs up the sky on a cobweb to an altitude of 3,000 feet. At that height you get a wide-angle view of the 10,000 square-mile Mackenzie delta, which is over a hundred miles long. The river splits into three channels at Point Separation farther south, then becomes an immense soggy blotting pad containing literally thousands of lakes–or perhaps thousands of islands, because land and water are so interwoven that you can't tell which is which. Seventy miles north of here is the Beaufort Sea, with oil exploration going on in both the delta and arctic waters beyond. West is the Richardson Mountain chain; under us a dozen geese homing to their summer nesting grounds.

We land on a dirt runway and trundle to a bumpy stop. Beside the field is a small log structure, about ten feet by twelve, which is apparently the airport terminal: Aklavik International Airport? I say goodbye to the Cessna pilot, who is scheduled to return for me this evening at eight. It's now 9:15 AM, so I have nearly eleven hours in which I can talk to people. But there is no one in sight, even though the Cessna landed close to the centre of Aklavik. Dick Hill had given me the name of the settlement-council chairman, Don McWatt, but I don't know where he lives. The whole community seems to be asleep, nothing moves. Only some formidable-looking husky dogs lift their heads as I walk past, and give me a sleepy evil eye: they don't like strangers.

At Aklavik, there are frame houses and trailers here and there, squatting in the mud; mounds of snow and ice, slowly melting in the 60° sun; tin cans and bottles along the boardwalk awaiting spring clean-up; and two graveyards in the town centre, with wooden crosses and markers surrounded by a white picket fence: *Dearly Beloveds* and *RIPs* cradled by water and mud. Mackie's General Store is locked and smokeless. The hotel-cum-restaurant has apparently never had a guest; the pool room is almost noisy with silence. There's a feeling of slight panic: I may walk these dirt streets all day long and never see a human face.

Two blocks away some native kids are walking. I hurry after them, but they disappear like smoke before I can catch up and ask directions to Don McWatt's house. It's like being born again into a world so different from the fat south that your mind works hard to adjust. I intrude past a sign that says "No Admittance" into the electric generating plant, where the man on duty tells me that Don McWatt lives in a white trailer, in a north-south-east-west direction from the river.

Don McWatt's place is completely silent, and I feel embarrassed at knocking and breaking into people's sleep. Some dogs in the willow brush behind make their displeasure known. But Don finally comes to the door sleepily.

Don is a Scotsman, a husky man in a T-shirt. He has a native wife and two children, works for the government, and does a little of everything to make a living. He thinks Aklavik is a great place to live, "At least I did until that thing happened a year ago. I thought this was the ideal place where you settle down and feel at home."

And he told me about the murder: it seems that this Eskimo kid got liquored up last year and killed a priest. Why? There is no certain answer to that question, except that in Aklavik most native people are on social assistance, welfare, call it what you like. The people are split roughly into three divisions, Loucheaux Indians, Eskimos, and whites. Some members of these racial groups mix socially, but many do not. Native teenagers don't know what to do with their time;

there is nothing that allows them to keep their self-respect, and most are handicapped by lack of training and education. Hunting, fishing, and trapping are the traditional occupations, but they don't provide a good living any more: not with the oil companies splashing money around lavishly and old native values disappearing quickly in this new world of the white man's north. So Don McWatt is worried over a possible explosion soon, one that will make his "ideal place to live" a battleground of racial warfare.

Neighbour Frank Rivet is sixty-eight, a veteran hunter and trapper with deep lines creasing both cheeks and a greying moustache. Frank won't allow me to use my cassette recorder, says his story is worth lots of money: "I can get thousands of dollars for it from a man in the States!" Well, then, can I make notes? It seems I can, yes. George Kuzzinie, an Indian friend of the family, comes calling. Both Frank and George agree that the Canadian Broadcasting Corporation is "the rottenest thing in the world. All the people here want to see murder, adventure, westerns. What do we get? Culture!" Their voices drip with digust.

Frank says that 500 caribou were killed and left to rot in the Coppermine country east of here. "There won't be any caribou left if that sort of thing keeps on," he says. George Kuzzinie agrees. A few years ago 275,000 muskrats were taken in the delta: this year, only 40,000. Things are bad all over. "But I have this beautiful agate," Frank says. "My agate has pictures inside it, a lot of pictures, inside the stone itself. I want a million dollars for it."

Frank looks at me. Well, I don't have a million dollars in my pocket, at least not right at this moment. Frank seems to feel that I ought to have that money and it's hard to explain to him that I don't. So I asked about racial tension.

He says, "The country belongs to everybody." Which is a pretty good answer, except that some people generally want more of it than others.

Joe Carnagursky is something else again. He and his wife Dinah are both twenty-nine; their new house is the finest in Aklavik. Joe is of Czech extraction, has been here eight years. Dinah's great grandfather was John Firth, a Hudson's Bay Company factor called the "King of the North," ruling over a lonely empire on the shores of the Arctic Sea before the century's turn. Dinah is part Loucheaux Indian, and her looks are somewhere between merely pretty and extremely beautiful. I kid her about entering a local beauty contest. She replies pertly that she'd never enter one–"then nobody else would have a chance." Joe and his brother operate Carn Construction, perhaps the biggest such outfit in the Territories.

I happened to have arrived here on the anniversary of Aklavik's murderous night a year ago. The circumstances of that night are still fresh in Joe's and Dinah's minds. One Peter Thrasher, an Alaska Eskimo now living in Aklavik, had received $805 in land settlement money on that date. He put most of it in the bank, bought some clothes and liquor at Inuvik, and gave his son twenty dollars. Whereupon the sixteen-year-old Eugene Lawrence Thrasher got very drunk, whether on his father's whisky or on local homebrew no one seems to know. He broke into the HBC store with an axe and stole a rifle, then made for the Catholic rectory. There he was overheard quarrelling loudly with Father Franche, a much-respected sixty-seven-year-old priest. Father Franche appears to have ejected Thrasher from the rectory. Once outside the young Eskimo fired a bullet through the closed door, wounding the old man seriously. Then he ran.

RCMP Constable Charles Bunting followed the crazed youngster toward some willows beside the river, fired three warning shots over his head, then was shot himself. Frank Rivet, an expert marksman, heard the bombardment, and heard the wounded policeman call, "Shoot him. He shot the priest."

Frank Rivet fired one shot, intending to disable the boy. The slug hit young Thrasher in the chest, killing him. And later that night, another sixteen-year-old, Charles Koe, a friend of Lawrence Thrasher's, got drunk and sprayed bullets into the settlement in all directions. Another constable, rushed in to Aklavik after the earlier shooting, killed Koe.

Three people died: Father Franche, Lawrence Thrasher, and Charles Koe.

Terror still haunts Aklavik from that night. Dinah Carnagursky thinks Frank Rivet should have brought down young Thrasher without killing him. Which, of course, is easy to say if you aren't on the scene yourself. Joe Carnagursky says Rivet could only see a small part of the boy's body, and had to bring him down the best way he could.

"And there's still a lot of racial tension here," Joe says. The Indian Brotherhood, the Métis Association, and COPE, the Eskimo organization, are all stirring up trouble. Native kids have nothing to do with themselves, no money or way to get it except by trapping muskrats.

After all this talk of hatred and murder, Dinah says, "I don't like whites!" And yet she is married to a wealthy white man, has many white friends, lives in the settlement's best house.

Peter Thrasher, father of the dead boy, is forty-seven, a man built along the lines of an Arctic Hercules run slightly to fat. He weighs 265 pounds, has a bad back, and is a diabetic. He works at Aklavik's fur garment shop. In Peter's kitchen kids scurry back and forth. Soon the whole Thrasher family is going into the bush on a picnic, to take advantage of the warm, sunny weather. I avoid mention of Peter's dead son, thinking that he must have talked about that more than he likes. I do ask him about racial tension. "There is none," he says flatly. More contradictions, a perfect maze of differing opinions.

Peter Thrasher went to mission school as a youngster, but his grandfather, Mingaksek, took him out of school at age fifteen to learn hunting, trapping, and wilderness survival. Mingaksek taught him everything. Once, when the boy nearly drowned in an Arctic river, his grandfather pulled him out and dosed him with homebrew to prevent pneumonia. Mingaksek was father and mother to Peter, since the boy's own mother died spitting blood when he was even younger. Peter followed the old man around everywhere, plainly worshipping him. Man and boy, the two could walk fifteen hours a day on their trapline and keep it up for weeks. As a man come to his full strength, Peter could take 800 pounds on his back and walk with it. Mingaksek died in 1964. Peter dug his grave above the permafrost.

Peter's son is dead, killed by Frank Rivet; Peter's daughter is in a mental hospital at Red Deer, Alberta, because she began to hate all white people after her brother's death; Peter himself is a diabetic with a bad back. Beyond my understanding, he seems to have adjusted to all this tragedy. In the northern world, where nearly everything has changed from the old days, in which roads and pipelines have altered migration patterns of game animals, with oil and gas exploration throughout the Arctic, Peter Thrasher has retained a humanity and warmth I could feel even as a complete stranger.

I walk among willows bordering the river, near the place where young Thrasher was killed. The banks are lined with steel plates against spring break-up, when ice chews at the soft land, sometimes breaking off fifty foot chunks of it, and carries the dissolving landscape north to the Beaufort Sea. Brown caribou skins rot among bottles and tin cans. Forty miles away the Richardson mountains lift white peaks to the western horizon. It is a country of such mixed squalor and grandeur, of violence and peace, that one comes to terms with it only on *its* terms. But white men have never done that, and the day of the hunter is almost over.

As I fly back to Inuvik in early evening, a solid wall of cloud is rolling in from the Beaufort Sea. Soon everything–man, beast, and mountains–will be covered by that huge overcoat. Glancing down some three hundred feet I see the small Cessna reflected on water, apparently trapped inside a circle of mist in which a rainbow is also trapped. At this moment Peter Thrasher and his family must be gathering up knives and forks and tablecloth and picnic lunch to escape the threatening sky.

Peter is a descendant of those long ago hunters venturing

along glacier-shadowed corridors of northern rivers, hunters of the mammoth and caribou, hunters of the bear. Those prehistoric Asian people moved eastward and the people of Europe moved westward during the long-past millennia, the two finally meeting just a few centuries ago on the eastern seaboard of North America. Westward explorations of Europeans, during the last 500 years, are known and mapped. Eastward migrations of Asians stopped long ago on this continent and turned south. But I have an inexplainable feeling –because of all these eastward and westward movements– that everyone may have been looking for everyone else on the face of the Earth. And that migrations and explorations might have deeper motives than the mere pursuit of food and profit: because humanity has always been searching for itself.

Harbour Deep

It is another country, this rock within the sea, Newfoundland. In remote outports the language is Elizabethan English, or a language as close to it as five hundred years past can echo into the twentieth century. A man like myself, used to the jargon of Americanized English in mid-Canada, listens to this speech with the despairing feeling that here is a land preserved out of time long past, and I am a foreigner. Not only in language, but also foreign to the life-rhythms of fishermen and pulpwood cutters. Those are the bread-and-butter basics of this other country that joined Canada in 1949, but that still remains essentially different. Only the baby bonus, UIC benefits, the CBC, and similar federal encroachments into the great island reach the surface of awareness, but they scarcely touch the pride of people who live and die beside the sea.

Harbour Deep is an outport on the east coast of the Great Northern Peninsula. When my wife and I set out for that place, neither of us knew what we were getting into there, except that it would be hard to get out of, since ships called at Harbour Deep once a week only. And there were no roads.

I had been given the name of Ches Pittman, the store-keeper; he'd been asked to arrange accommodation for a few days. We met him on the Department of Transport dock after leaving the CN ship: a middle-aged man in a base-ball cap, with the unmistakable look of a man in charge. A free enterpriser to end all free enterprisers, he once said to me, "Put me down any place on Earth, and in a few hours I'll find a way to make money." I believe him.

Mountains and water surround Harbour Deep. Orange Bay sweeps in blue for several miles through a notch be-tween green mountains, exploring half a dozen smaller coves and bays. The village itself is a necklace of houses strung along three miles of a single road and causeway be-tween sea and mountains: road where there's room for houses, causeway where sheer cliffs crowd out the people. No police or fire department, no doctor. All is surrounded by a great quiet that finally, when your ears get used to it, breaks down into the small sounds of wind and waves, and of your own breathing body informing you that your life continues. Population a little over 400, with about six fami-lies predominating.

Over the 128 years that Harbour Deep has been in exist-ence these original families have increased, and Ropsons, Cassells, Loders, Pittmans, Pollards, Elgars, and Randells outnumber all the others. In fact, the whole village has in-termarried since its long-ago beginning, to the degree that just about everyone is liable to be the ninety-eighth cousin of just about everyone else, give or take a cousin and in-law or two. They are related in other ways as well, despite the psychological split between older generation and younger; the nineteenth century still lingers inside the shapes and forms of the twentieth. The teenagers in "the theatre," play-ing pool near a pot-bellied stove, drinking beer, and neck-ing, deafening rock music crowding every square inch of the building: these near-children clustering together for mutual dream-comfort are still the sons and daughters of fishermen whose working life is essentially an aloneness of water and distant sky.

We're sitting in a room at Ernie Cassell's house. "You'd better change those pants," my wife says. "Everybody will know you're from somewhere else, wearing those loud checked pants." She knows best almost always, but she's a little off-base this time.

"Of course I'm from somewhere else; everybody here knows that already."

We go to Pittman's store to buy some things, including a notebook and a package of cigarette tobacco.

"Oh, you roll your own, eh?" Ches Pittman says. I had anticipated just such a reaction, and hoped my expression didn't change while building a beautiful roll-your-own in four seconds flat. Ches Pittman looked at me with new respect.

We walked onto Pittman's dock, away from the half-ton GMC pickup with three flat tires, used for hauling gravel on the road when its tires aren't flat. Boats are chugging in from the sea, for the salmon season is in full swing; from early June to about July 20 Pittmans, Pollards, Elgars, and all the rest bring in their catch. And for every week of salmon fishing Ches Pittman hands out one unemployment insurance stamp. Which is an interesting point, because you need twelve stamps to get UIC benefits during the long winter. Salmon fishing gives you six; for every 600 pounds of herring during the May season, one stamp; and 400 pounds of cod, one stamp. If you're good or lucky or both you can make this add up to twelve stamps without trouble.

However, only the merchant—and here that's Ches Pittman—can give you those UIC stamps. Therefore you can't sell your fish to anyone else, even at a much higher price: you're locked-in to the merchant, or else you and your family will not receive UIC benefits the following winter. The sign in front of Pittman's store and dock says: "With reference to salmon price: We are prepared to meet or best any competition provided in this area." But there is no competition this side of Englee, thirty miles distant. Last winter there was also Charlie Murcill, who'd been running a store and buying fish for forty years. But Murcill has cancer, and is now retired. The price for large salmon is a dollar a pound, and seventy-five cents for small. Some think the price would be higher if Ches Pittman had any competition.

Talking with Richard Ropson, a brown, middle-aged fisherman, on his landing stage, he mentions that occasionally a finback whale will break through the salmon nets: "It do happen," he says, "yiss, but not very often, sir." Richard caught eighty salmon in his nets that day, but another Ropson caught 110.

Ernest Walters, eighty, retired schoolmaster, came to Harbour Deep fifty years ago, and married a local girl. Bent, white-haired, and a little feeble, he runs a small store in South West Bottom, which is three miles away along the road and causeway from North West Bottom at the opposite end of the village. Walters is also Justice of the Peace. When I asked him about any local wrong-doing, he says that the crime-wave hereabouts is pretty picayune: such things as young fellows getting drunk on beer, or infractions of the game laws. Walters leaves prosecutions to the magistrate from St. Anthony, who visits Harbour Deep twice a year.

Diane Elgar, in her mid-thirties, is the community nurse. She answered a Grenfell Mission advertisement in England and came here eight years ago. "I wanted adventure," she says. Adventure consists of pulling teeth, bandaging axe wounds, and attending to snowmobile accidents in winter. She is also educated as a midwife. In case of a really serious medical problem, she phones Dr. Tuton in St. Anthony, and he can get here within a few minutes by aeroplane. But the telephone itself came to Harbour Deep only last December; when accidents happened twenty years ago, the only way a sick or injured person could reach St. Anthony was by dog team.

The yearly incomes of fishermen range all the way from $3,000 to $20,000. The disparity is explainable only in terms of the differences in people, equipment, and fishing know-how. However, $3,000 in Harbour Deep would be equivalent to $8,000 or $10,000 a year in, say, Toronto. There is no property tax here; and even the poorest fisherman will have a refrigerator, a deep freeze, and television by satellite. Behind the village a mountain is wired for sound and pictures; sprouting television aerials arch among black spruce and tamarack.

The old men do not watch television much; they walk the long road between the two village Bottoms; they talk to each other, remembering the old days when there were no power boats, and you had to row fifteen miles to erect underwater fences in the sea to catch salmon; and sea-days of pulling at oars where the undersea currents were strong rivers criss-crossing under the waves. And then the salmon sold for only a few cents a pound. The hot summer sun preserves a pale memory of their once deep-mahogany faces.

They are playing pool at the theatre, the teenagers and sub-teenagers, when I visit the place. Beer is swigged, loud music plays, and I am three times the age of any teenager there. A few boys work for the hydro, a few help their fathers fish, but most leave the village, because Harbour Deep will not support more than its present forty fishing boats. Only a limited number of fishing areas is available, and each man draws his own by lot before the fishing season opens. And for girls there is nothing but schoolteaching or helping out at one of the stores. They must get married, or leave, and most do leave. But when people leave, something is lost out of themselves. This little beyond-the-end-of-anywhere outport has its own leisurely and fierce attraction. Some of them remember; some of them come back during holidays for a few hot weeks of summer.

Noah Pittman, now in his failing eighties, remembers the villages before this village. More than fifty years ago the people of Harbour Deep were scattered among the half-dozen coves around Orange Bay: Duggan's Cove, Jack's Cove, and several others. But came a voice from on high, which in this case was the M.J. Mooney Lumber Company, operating a mill at North East Bottom and employing many fishermen to cut pulpwood. The voice said: move yourselves and all your goods and chattels close to the mill, live there in a place most convenient to your employers. Lo and behold the people listened. They tore down their houses, laid each wall across two boats, and rowed them several miles to the present site of Harbour Deep.

The people came, all of them moved–except Noah Pittman's father. He refused–stubbornly, some of his neighbours thought–to obey the new masters. He kept on fishing as his father had done, while the rest abandoned the sea, allowing their nets and boats to rot beside the shore. But there came a day in the 1920s when the M.J. Mooney mill burned to a heap of ashes and closed down operations; and stubborn old Pittman was the only man still fishing. The villagers were forced to turn again to the sea for a living, learn the old trade all over again, and mend damaged nets and caulk their sun-bleached boats along the shore. Perhaps it occurred to them at the time that some virtue may reside in stubbornness, some pride and perhaps some vision.

Surrounded by high green mountains, Harbour Deep's present location has much less level garden land than the old villages had; you could even escape the sun there, and sometimes wander off into cool green forests. But M.J. Mooney and all his works are gone now, save for a pair of rusty boilers squatting like sentinels near the water of North East Bottom. House foundations, lost children's toys, and even graveyards are impossible to find, overgrown with grass and underbrush; the old people who were ancestors of Ropsons, Cassells, Pittmans, Pollards, and Elgars remain there, like stubborn ghosts beside the sea.

During our stay at Harbour Deep we lived with Ernie and Bella Cassell: she vivid and bustling about her household tasks; he a small man in his mid-fifties, not taciturn exactly, but given to silences and periods of abstraction. Often after brewis (a Newfoundland dish of cod, boiled bread, beef, pork, and spices all mixed together) is served for lunch, with Bella talking to my wife over the teacups, I have seen Ernie build a cigarette and then slowly lean forward behind his wife's body, his mind disappearing altogether into a place where none of us can follow. I twist in my chair to watch him go, his face still having the semblance of being here, like a hostage left behind. It is both commonplace and mysterious, this disappearance.

Pleman Pollard, called "Ple" by his friends, is Ernie's fishing partner. Ple is also in his mid-fifties, eyes flashing behind bottle-bottom glasses—a volatile and sociable wordslinger in direct contrast to Ernie's silent departures. All fishermen have partners; work against wind and wave is too hard for one man alone.

On the fishing stage at 5 AM, they prepare again and again for the continual expeditions outward that make up their lives. Between gateway mountains the sun is soon to appear in a narrow slot that designates the open sea. Ernie and Ple Pollard chug eastward to tend their nets and bring back salmon. Both are in character: Ernie is no doubt silent, Ple chattering. The round trip takes upwards of four hours, and is repeated twice a day. The two boats they operate were built by themselves, except for inboard diesel motors, also repaired by themselves if necessary. All their equipment, except the two-hundred-dollar, fifty-fathom nylon nets, is furnished by their own ingenuity. In fact, every fisherman in Harbour Deep builds his own boat.

We'd been at the village for three days when the first wedding in three years took place. Of course, other marriages of Harbour Deep people had occurred "outside," but this one was cause for local celebration. Melvin Cassell, twenty-six, and Drusilla Randell, nineteen, are the principals. Father Shepherd, from Jackson's Arm, is scheduled to arrive by boat to perform the nuptials in late afternoon at the Anglican Church. Afterwards everyone will jam the Orange Hall for a reception, complete with food and beer.

I heard someone say about Drusilla: "We're going to marry her up"—but time passed and Father Shepherd did not appear. It was 8 PM when he did arrive and the ceremony finally took place. Flashbulbs flashed as cameras recorded the moment when pale bride and slightly red-faced groom appeared at the church door. Several small boys and girls stood by with green switches cut from trees, which I thought at first represented some hangover from druidical rituals, until the flies attacked. Those flies divided into para-military squads of about forty, the better to concentrate separately on arms and legs and faces of wedding guests. Two friends of the groom lurked, fly-bitten, with shotguns in bushes outside the church. The guns boomed like a sudden God on Moses' mountain, and everyone jumped. The little black flies, locally called "skits," desisted not in their bloody work.

Back at Ernie's house, I am seeking refuge from the skits. Ple Pollard enters, having partaken of at least one beer. Ple talks, my wife and I listen. Another man enters the kitchen, then a boy. All of us listen. Maybe it's Elizabethan English, maybe Newfoundlandese: but I understand about six words in ten, leaving me minus four, which I have my wife translate later.

"I loves fishing," Ple says, "but I hates working in the woods." That's the bare gist of it, but doesn't convey Ple's hypnotic outport bravura, which leaves me genuinely spellbound, and also slightly humiliated that I can't join this paean of thanksgiving to sun and sea and being alive.

Next morning at 9 AM, Ernie is still waiting patiently for his partner on the fishing stage; Ple has imbided a little too much the night before. But then, a man who can so intoxicate with words should be forgiven a little alcohol.

One incident from forty years before overrides all others in the history of Harbour Deep. It concerns Joseph and Elijah Cassell, two brothers who were jigging for cod in Orange Bay. A giant finback whale surfaced near their small boat. Elijah screamed, either from fear or out of hope that he might scare off the beast. A huge tail smashed into the boat, crushing Elijah's neck and most of his ribs. He sank, weighted down by his heavy seaboots. But Joseph clung to the ruined boat, yelling for help.

When other fishermen rescued him, the whale was long

gone. They used cod jiggers to grapple for Elijah's body, with hooks scraping the bottom in forty fathoms of water; but without result. Finally Uncle Jim Randell noticed Elijah's jigger hanging from the wrecked boat.

"He'll know that jigger," said Uncle Jim, retrieving it and dropping the big hooks far down. And Elijah did know his own jigger, for Uncle Jim hooked something, the sleeve and hand of a dead man. Elijah emerged from the sea, dragged upward by one arm, his body twisting from side to side on the cod-jigging line, head waving slackly on its broken neck.

"He didn't look too good," Ernie Cassell remembers.

A shiver ran through the village forty years ago. Elijah was buried in the graveyard. Joseph, the survivor, now quite deaf and nearly eighty, still lives in Harbour Deep.

Around him the Pollards, Cassells, Pittmans, Ropsons, Garlands, Elgars – all of them – live non-fiction lives in their village, like other people in town and country and city; they are human, they are born and they die. And we are involved with all of them, in ways I can't explain. But perhaps when the cities die, one by one, drowned in their own garbage, and when fresh-water lakes are choked with floating slime, men and women who can whittle survival from a piece of driftwood may still be living in villages beside the sea. Not idyllic lives, certainly; but they will survive as Joseph survived – close to the jaws of a monster whale.

Argus in Labrador

On the morning of February 6, 1975, two hunters set out from the coastal Eskimo village of Nain in Labrador to trap foxes on Dog Island, a few miles offshore. Their names were Jacko Onalik and Martin Senigak, ages twenty-four and fifty. They took no food along on their blue snowmobile, since they were intending to return to Nain that same night. By next morning they still hadn't shown up at Nain, and their families were alarmed. Friends went out to look for them, but found only the tracks of Jacko's and Martin's blue snowmobile. The tracks ended at an open lead in the water.

The RCMP detachment at Nain immediately radioed the Canadian Forces' Maritime Headquarters in Halifax, which sent a Buffalo Search and Rescue aircraft to look for the two lost hunters. Snowmobiles from that Eskimo village, 300 miles north of Newfoundland, also combed Labrador coastal waters; at this season the water was covered with ice for miles out into the North Atlantic. And a helicopter from Squadron 413 at Summerside, PEI, was dispatched to the scene. Without result. Jack Onalik and Martin Senigak were still missing.

5 AM, February 12: I'm at the Canadian Forces Base in Greenwood, Nova Scotia, with an Argus aircrew from Squadron 405, listening to coastal weather reports in the briefing room. And feeling rather bewildered at the rapid pace of events. Crew captain Major Ken Keir outlines the operation. He is a grey veteran with 9,000 hours flying time, who comes from Victoria, British Columbia. Today's flight would normally be a fisheries patrol, on which foreign trawlers operating outside or illegally inside the Canadian twelve-mile limit would be monitored and photographed. But Jacko and Martin were an added factor. The village elders of Nain had asked that Search and Rescue try one more time. The two men might still be alive, floating on an ice-pan broken off from the shore ice. And they could have taken seal for food – might even be awaiting rescue at this very moment.

"But there's still another complication," Major Keir told the aircrew. An American DC7, flying from Prestwick, England to Gander, Newfoundland, was now reported far off course – 115 miles from Sable Island with only three hours' fuel left in its tanks. The DC7's navigation equipment must have gone completely haywire for the plane to have strayed so far south. There was now a strong possibility that it might be forced down in the sea.

A little later, Greenwood radio relayed the message that the American plane was 130 miles from Sydney, Nova Scotia. We scrub the DC7, and are free to search for Jacko and Martin. And afterwards, if there was time, we could prowl around the Strait of Belle Isle, overseeing foreign fishing trawlers.

The Argus aircraft itself is the principal character in this story, apart from the two Eskimos. When sixteen military crewmen and two civilians boarded it on a snow-covered field around 6 AM, the thing looked enormous. And it is just that. One hundred and twenty-eight feet long, its wingspan wider than the tallest building in my hometown, it has an airframe by Canadair, with four prop-driven Pratt and Whitney engines. Unlike anonymous airline jets that all look the same to me, the Canadian Argus might be said to possess much the same character as that of its fellow countrymen. Slow and reliable, its cruising speed is only 180 to 220 miles an hour, but an Argus can stay in the air more than twenty-four hours if necessary. In service since 1958, and soon to be replaced by more modern aircraft, only one Argus has ever been lost: during Canadian-American exercises off Puerto Rico several years back. Ron Lasseter, today's tactical co-ordinator, says of that plane, "It may have been flying too low, looking for submarines, and caught one wingtip in the water." Fifteen Canadians died on that Argus, in the sea off Puerto Rico.

While the three pilots go through all the complicated rigmarole of getting the sky-buggy ready for 7 AM take-off, boyish-looking Capt. Lasseter shows me around the aircraft. I am slightly excited – well, maybe a little more than slightly. But all the military guys around me look calm and collected; it's nearly everyday stuff to them. The radio men check equipment; the navigators are about to navigate; the engineers see to their gauges and dials and things. And the three pilots, sitting in the big flightdeck among so many gimmicks that no single Rube-Goldberg brain could have conceived them all – the pilots look ordinary! And Ron Lasseter, from Huntsville, Ontario, is like a tour guide for me. He shows me everything but the secret stuff, which is canvas-covered. I don't know what it is, and don't want to know; but I harbour the hope that we have an electronic bug implanted in every foreign trawler's rear end.

On a more commonplace level, the Argus has all the household equipment normally found in a well-furnished apartment. Galley with an electric stove and frypan, toaster and frig; also radar, radio, and other communications gadgets not found in any home. And a chemical toilet, which is one step ahead of my own primitive rural outhouse. There are seats and bunks where you can flake out if flight-fatigue gets to you; also white paper bags, which Ron Lasseter says are for airsickness. The aircrew, if any of them do happen to get sick from too much aerobatics, just use the bags provided and go back to their jobs immediately; there's a pride involved in not having someone else take on the job you're supposed to do yourself. And among all the calm bustle around me, only the observers seem to be not quite so occupied as the rest. They've got nothing to observe yet, not until take-off. Which reminds me that Argus, in Greek mythology, had a hundred eyes, of which only two could sleep at one time. When we are air-borne, none of our human and electronic eyes will fall asleep.

7:20 AM: Take-off time (and I feel very melodramatic about it)—187,000 pounds of old-and-tired-from-years-of-service Argus lumber into the air above our planet. Unfastening my seatbelt, I stand behind Major Keir and Capt. Bob Fuller, noticing the worn condition of the Argus' padded instrument panel, noticing also with some surprise the American flag badge on Bob Fuller's shoulder. He's an American exchange officer from Glendale, California, on a two-year tour of duty in Canada. His counterpart is somewhere in the United States with the American military—a portable Canadian branch plant. Bob Fuller is a most likeable guy, and no doubt helps out with his abundant American know-how.

We are some 8,000 feet high, crossing over the Summerside Search and Rescue base, then above the Strait of Belle Isle between Newfoundland and Quebec. Under us ice and snow and more ice and snow. Paul Gelinas, a photographer, is dashing hither and yon making little rapturous noises and taking pictures. I circulate the hundred-foot cigar tube and talk to people. We are all dressed in bulky flying suits, and later rubberized orange Mae West lifejackets, each stuffed with a variety of survival equipment, in case of being forced down in the sea. I think of Jacko and Martin down there, for whom this mission of ours might mean life itself.

Breakfast is bacon and eggs, served on disposable plates to the accompaniment of four engines so noisy that you almost have to spit in someone's ear before your voice is audible. Grey dawn arrives without the prior announcement of a red sunrise: it's just here. Urgency and excitement subside, the dentist's drill of noise and vibration continues. I lie on the reclining seats, mulling over the general pattern of Canadian Forces' patrol operations. There are four main types of flights: Northern Patrols, Fisheries Patrols, Search and Rescue, plus the all-important Ocean Surveillance Patrols. Helicopters, Buffalos, and the amphibious Albatross are employed for long-range Search and Rescue, and the general-purpose Argus for all four types of operations. Sovereignty is, of course, involved: the necessity of being on the spot and saying implicitly to foreign trawlers and the occasional ship traversing our North West Passage: this is Canadian territory.

Anyway, I'm trying to get CanFor patrol operations straight and clear in my mind. It calls for tracing out a mental map of Canada, on which the long-range Argus flies north and west from the big Greenwood base to Frobisher Bay and Yellowknife in the central Arctic. And at the same time Maritime West planes from Comox, BC, fly north and east just inside the Canadian boundary from Alaska, also arriving at Yellowknife. They form a kind of giant pincers, covering the entire Canadian Arctic. The reasons for these flights involve much more than sovereignty: caribou herd counts, whale in the Beaufort Sea, movements of Indian and Eskimo peoples, possible military threat from across the polar regions, and much more.

In summer there are two Northern Patrols a month. In winter, eastern operations are limited to the area around Frobisher Bay on Baffin Island, for a variety of reasons. The only hardtop airfields in the eastern Arctic are at Frobisher and Thule, Greenland (the latter an American base). Therefore, a suitable landing field in the central Arctic, perhaps at Resolute Bay, is an absolute necessity for both winter and summer operations. Another factor inhibiting all flights is the amount of fuel available: the Argus swills a great deal of its scarce and expensive 115 to 145 octane gasoline; big commercial jets and foreign military aircraft fly on a cheaper mixture. In addition, all "operational employment" – meaning the activities of both ships and aircraft – was reduced 30 per cent in 1975, because of defence budget restrictions and a cutback in military personnel. Search and Rescue is still given first priority, but nevertheless this reduction in operational employment is spread over all the different types of operations. It means that the poverty-stricken Canadian Forces are crippled by lack of men and money. It's a curious paradox that we waste millions of dollars on such things as egg spoilage, the Hamilton Harbour corruption affair, and all our proliferating bureaucracy – but can't scrape up enough money to permit adequate Search and Rescue operations to save human lives, or sufficient northern patrols to preserve the national boundaries of Canada.

There's no way that you can get to know sixteen men in a sixteen-hour period of time, especially with those four Pratt and Whitneys yammering away like mad dogs. Climbing down into the Argus' plexiglas nose, my flesh feeling precarious and my bones very breakable, apparently surrounded by white sub-Arctic wasteland, I hear someone say on my radio headset, "Cover up that American flag, Bob. It's not that we don't love you, but . . . "

And someone else says, "Doesn't matter, they've already photographed it." I wonder if that dialogue was meant for me. Who's kidding who?

Aircrew hometowns range from one side of the country to the other. Capt. Bob Blouin, navigator from Quebec City, was in on the search and rescue of Marten Hartwell a few years back. So was Warrant Officer Rod Skanes, flight engineer from Bell Island, Newfoundland, with twenty-five years' service in the Canadian Forces. (Marten Hartwell was the small-plane pilot who went down north of Yellowknife and survived until rescue by chewing on some of his dead passengers.) Corporal Glen Hooge, observer from Thompson, Manitoba, and now Victoria, British Columbia, was originally in the army artillery before re-mustering to aircrew.

Captain Mike Gibbons, navigator from London, Ontario, was British-born. Gibbons is a greying veteran, now thirty-nine, previously stationed with Squadron 415 at Summerside. He's been involved in so many rescue flights that he can't remember them all: tankers breaking up in heavy seas, people floating in lifejackets, the pontooned Albatross landing in grey stucco waves to pick up survivors. He does remember Albert Muse, a fisherman in the Gulf of St. Lawrence. Muse's fishing trawler was awash in heavy seas in weather so rough that he tied himself to the mast in order not to be swept overboard. All other crew members were already drowned. Sighting the rescue aircraft, he untied himself. Mike well remembers Albert's first words over the radio to his rescuers: "Well jeez, boy, I'll tell ya, it's some wet down here!"

Mike tells me about the MA-1 rescue kits, consisting of a long rope hung with survival items and a life raft at either end. One raft is dropped, then the other, after which wind and waves cause the two rafts to encircle floating survivors. In the old RCAF days at Summerside, it was much more difficult to rescue fishermen in distress. They would take long chances, fishing far out from shore, and in bad weather might be swept 300 miles into the Atlantic. They seldom had a radio, which made things difficult for Search and Rescue. Of course, radio now is standard equipment, unless you're competing in the Nanaimo Bathtub Derby.

10:30 AM: We're roaring above Labrador, a mottled wasteland of granite and ice, so grim in aspect that it resembles "the bourne from which no traveller returns." Geologists say it's so old that it contains no fossil remnants of plants or animals. The Argus swoops low over Nain, an Eskimo village, surrounded by cliffs and mountains. Nain is composed of perhaps a hundred or so government prefab houses. The Argus radio is in touch with the RCMP down there.

East of the mainland village we begin our dog-leg sweeps, thirty miles in one direction, then back on an opposite course four miles distant from our previous swing but flying parallel to it. This allows two-mile visibility on either side of the aeroplane. Observers at side windows and in the nose scan the ice for anything unusual, anything that moves, anything alive. But there is nothing. Once, on a sweep over Dog Island, I catch sight of two wooden houses, no doubt gathered and painstakingly built from driftwood. Their chimneys are smokeless. They appear as deserted as the remains of stone houses built by Norsemen on this coast a thousand years ago.

Below is the unimaginable vastness of ice: ice in mosaic patterns of break-up and re-freezing, ice in jagged pressure ridges, ice surrounding open black rapiers of cold water. The twenty Eskimo words for snow must be multiplied a dozen times to reach the sum total of names for different kinds of ice. And 300 feet up seems perilously close to the frozen Earth we came from, and to which we must not return too abruptly. Three times we sight small groups of caribou that have come over the ice to these stone islands searching for caribou moss and lichens. And of course there might be the occasional polar bear, white wanderers in their white world.

1:30: In the galley cooking steaks, I say to Ken Keir, "They must be goners; it's six days now since they went missing."

He stared at his paper plate a moment, then said quietly, "You know, I'd like to think that if I were down there, everyone would be doing their damnedest."

At 2:15 it is evident that our damnedest isn't enough. In three and a half hours we have criss-crossed, cross-examined, and in effect placed 2,000 square miles of the North Atlantic under our Argus microscope. All around stretches the vague misty horizon, blending white ice and sky of palest blue. Nothing moves there but a few caribou, bear, and seal; nothing else lives. There is nothing for us to do but radio the RCMP detachment at Nain. They will talk to the village elders, explain our failure. I hope that the village people understand: we tried our best.

Swinging around in a great circle, we head south toward fishing grounds near the Strait of Belle Isle. After the slow speed of low flying, acceleration is like hornets buzzing in my ears. On the flightdeck, staring at hundreds of dials and gauges, I am fascinated by the engine monitor. There's an electronic stethoscope implanted in every spark plug, making green fluorescence twinkle under glass, remote from the plugs themselves. All medical devices for monitoring the human body must be parallelled here in a man-made aeroplane; qualified experts like these pilots can name them all. We are watching the plane's entire equipment with an electronic spy. And, watching everything, it makes you wonder: who is watching us?

A sudden radar blip from something fourteen miles away. Russian trawler or alien invaders from Mars? The Argus banks, my body weight appears to double and then triple, I weigh about 600 pounds and hold onto something that moves under my hand. It's Ron Lasseter and he grins. Below us the towers and turrets of a great white castle are flashing past.

"Radar can't tell the difference between icebergs and ships," Ron says.

Another iceberg. "Aha, did that thing ever fool you," I jibe at the radar absentmindedly, while Ron is talking. He's telling me about the Russian trawler caught inside our twelve-mile limit a few months ago, unhurriedly taking up lobster traps. I think: the nerve of those guys! If we ever did that in the Sea of Okhotskkamchatka, they'd demand Baffin Island for compensation.

"We photographed them," Ron says, "and let their government see the pictures. The Russians apologized."

I am mollified.

The plane swoops down again, with Ron acting as tour-guide of the ice floes. "These Russian factory ships run to 8,-000 tons, their trawlers several times bigger than ours. We take their pictures, stare at them eyeball to eyeball, photographing them photographing us photographing them." I'm getting dizzy from this description, staring down at cameras and electronic spies and thinking, "Am I imagining myself imagining myself or is someone else doing it?" The giant Argus banks south, its hundred eyes shuttered, their work finished.

5:30: Bright weather has changed to grey mist outside. Somewhere west of us the sun seeds a thousand miles of cloud to orangy red, streaking the long horizon. We are homing to Greenwood Base. Monotony and tedium seep into the mind, which I didn't feel when outward bound. Three or four crew members flake out in bunks, others heat soup in the galley as Major Keir drives the big Argus steadily south. I am half-lying, feet braced against an aluminum partition, thinking about all this: this exclusively male world, because no women are aircrew, jobs that might be combat roles in future. Although Greenwood does have many women in uniform, both commissioned and non-com-(batant).

9 PM: I am awakened by someone shouting in my ear that we may have a landing overshoot. We do not—and touch the runway like 187,000 pounds of feathers floating in no wind. And there is this deafening silence from engine stoppage, an absence of sound that rings in my head after being a day-long citizen of the sky-world. My ears are still adjusting during de-briefing. But while we're in the mess, with yellow beer at table, the crew talking together casually, those four Pratt and Whitney engines recede to a silent snow-covered hangar elsewhere.

Beer begins to relax the tension, and I am aware after the

fact that there has been tension. Major Chuck Smith, from another aircrew, talks about the need for more Northern Patrols and Search and Rescue capabilities. Military jargon again, but how else to refer to it? He tells me about the world air routes criss-crossing the Arctic; and how someday there's likely to be a godawful air disaster there, with 300 people crashed but alive, lost in those immense distances.

"And I've counted sixty-two Russian trawlers in one ten-mile area," he says. "During the season, several hundred foreign ships are trespassing on our continental shelf." I ask him if he thinks we should have a hundred-mile limit for Canadian waters. Chuck looks at me wryly.

"It's like this: you can have a village speed limit of twenty miles an hour, but that makes no difference at all if you don't have a village cop to enforce it." Cynical or not, the inference is unmistakable: if we don't control Canadian waters ourselves, the vacuum will be occupied by others.

Greenwood Base is slumbering toward midnight. Beyond snow-covered runways the hundred-eyed Argus sleeps in its hangar. Its crew straggles off to bed; the bar closes. And I am tired, the adventure almost over. Jacko Onalik's and Martin Senigak's life adventure is almost certainly ended, too. The only comfort for the living is to know that we did our best. And, hopefully, at the next report of sailors in lifejackets afloat in the North Atlantic, or of other Jackos or Martins lost from their northern settlements, the Argus or its sky-successor may arrive at the scene in time.

"Her Gates Both East and West"

On the road again: 1971. Sometimes it seems I've been wandering most of my life. Come to think of it, maybe wandering is my life: the last days at home in a fever to get away, the mind seeing places you want to go to superimposed on your own backyard. Of course, travelling is as much fun anticipating as doing—watching the distance shorten under blurred car wheels, or finally getting there and matching what you have in your head with the real thing. And when inward imaginings and outward reality rush together at sixty miles an hour, you gain something that can't be bought—except with the time of your life.

My wife and I hitched a five-year-old trailer to our car that summer and drove through western Canada, hopping from one province to another whenever something interested us: riding around a Saskatchewan farm on a red, roaring combine; fantasizing over dinosaur fossils in Alberta. By the time we got back to Ontario it was getting cold, so I continued across the country alone by train and plane.

Thinking about the whole trip after I returned was like watching one of those jumpy old movies with the mind's eye. You know the kind: the picture jerks unexpectedly from scene to scene and place to place. For it was a journey of the mind as well as of miles, which means I can go back there any time. . . .

British Columbia

Maybe it's a flaw in my character, but I love Vancouver. I've been broke there, worked in factories there, picked blackberries on False Creek there, and been desperate there. The whole city is an adventure – the lush lotusland of the Fraser delta, where drunks pass out on evergreen lawns in winter and don't freeze: they just lie there until spring and peacefully mildew. And I have friends in Vancouver, some of them more or less level-headed, despite the Jaycee euphoria of the place. Reluctantly, they manage to forgive me for living somewhere else. So we park the trailer at a friend's house in suburban Burnaby for a few days.

A week later we're cutting across the waist of Vancouver Island, heading west toward Tofino and Ucluelet on a road so steep that the mountain goats all have psychiatrists. Mist hangs in upper reaches of stone; trees farther down visibly change colour to pale pea-green or dark grass-green as mist thins or thickens. It is, of course, magnificent. We stop at an unlevel place beside the road for lunch. A narrow mile-a-minute river has carved solid rock into a tortuous honeycombed maze. We eat sandwiches with bananas for dessert. I say, "Let's buy some land here and build a house!" (I have visions of merging my lesser nature into a larger Nature and being as creative as hell.)

The island's west coast between Ucleulet and Tofino is a marvellous thirty miles of level golden sand. Whales lollop, spouting a few miles out from our parking spot. I say, "Let's buy some land!"

Anything that's any good you always want to own yourself, to be able to have it and see it again and again. That is, until you really think about it. It's taken me a long time to learn that anything marvellous – all those things that produce an emotion in your throat – why, I own those things already. The eyes take title and the mind possesses. That's not just writer's rhetoric. The act of appreciation doesn't constitute legal ownership, but nevertheless it embodies the knowledge that a human being is composed of all the things that he has seen and known and loved.

Just the same, when driving east later through high and wide Glacier National Park, I say, "Let's buy a goddam mountain!"

Alberta

From Brooks, Alberta (about 140 miles east of Calgary), we drive forty miles north to the dinosaur park. Fertile plains of wheat country give way to a moon landscape of grey skull-like hills in ghostly sunshine. Here, where ancient volcanoes spattered sky and earth with ashes long ago, the Red Deer River pushes its green wedge through nearly dead earth. Soon we're standing with other sightseers outside a large glass case containing a fossilized dinosaur skeleton, listening to the park warden's spiel.

Eighty million years ago a body of water 500 miles wide, called the "Bearpaw Sea" by geologists, split our whole continent from the Gulf of Mexico to the Arctic Ocean. That was in late afternoon of the day of the dinosaurs. Those overgrown lizards lived on the edge of that ancient sea when Alberta was semitropical. The carnivores among them—reptiles from five to forty feet long—roamed the land masses before the Rocky Mountains were born. The vegetarians, generally smaller in Alberta, were semiaquatic beasts, feeding on plants and prehistoric green salad in the marshlands.

One particular dinosaur of that early era was a duckbilled vegetarian, some twenty-five feet long. I call him Albert, giving him a human handle to make the huge reptile less alien. Consider Albert. There he is, body half submerged in water, eating greens and being completely at home in the sunlit landscape of ancient Earth. Albert probably had a personality—gentle, I think, and perhaps patient. Under a blue sky and bright white sun, chewing, chewing, chewing. No hint of danger from earth or water.

Then death appeared in the form of carnivorous Tyranno-saurus Rex, who was thirty-five feet long. He grabbed Albert's tail with teeth like ivory traps. Albert struggled, of course, and escaped eventually into deep water, mooing plaintively.

From that time on Albert's good disposition was ruined. His broken tail took a long time to heal, but it did, although aching continually. When he died much later, that tail was a primary reason. For Albert couldn't swim as well, and had to be cautious about shallow water; thus the more tender plants remained out of reach. His digestion and nervous system were also probably ruined; his love-life became a nightmare. And when he died, moon tides swept his body back to the edge of the Bearpaw Sea. It rotted there, and earth, a slow brown-green blanket, formed around Albert's skeleton.

I stand outside a glass case near Brooks, Alberta, in 1971, and there's Albert's skeleton, his tail still bearing marks of Tyrannosaurus' teeth after eighty million years. His bones are now completely fossilized, organic matter replaced with elements of earth. Only shape and form remain. But there's Albert still.

Saskatchewan

Wilf McKenzie is a wheat farmer ("I'd rather go broke than do anything else!") near Moose Jaw, Saskatchewan—he's red-faced, forthright, and a consummate free enterpriser ("Don't like government handouts, never did!"): a man who thinks that the farmer's biggest problem is marketing.

"Look," he says, as the red, roaring combine grumbles around his 1,000 acres and I hold onto the railing, "we grow wheat for the world, food for the hungry, and there's something wrong when that food can't be sold."

For miles and miles in all directions the only thing you can see is bright yellow wheat. I bawl hoarsely into Wilf McKenzie's ear, "Okay, it's the good life for you, but why?"

Spinning the big Massey-Ferguson around, he says,

"Well, freedom for instance, close to nature and all that. My father homesteaded this section and a half, and now it's me. I've got no sons, but my daughter's husband will run the place after I'm gone."

"You mean tradition?"

"Yes, there's that. And what it says in the Bible, that man was made from dust, and from this same dust we take food for the world."

I look around at the sunlit miles of "dust," heavy clay soil laid down here on the edge of the Regina Plain when the last glaciers scrunched past nearly 20,000 years ago.

"But you're lucky," I say. "You inherited this place. So will your son-in-law. What about the kids who grow up today and in the future? They tell me it takes $100,000 worth of land and machinery to start a kingdom like this one. Say a young guy gets married and he and his wife want to be wheat farmers. How can they raise all that cash?"

Wilf replies so softly over the machine's roar that I have to bend close to his sunburned sixtyish face. "There isn't any way *that* kid can ever be a farmer," he says. "It's a kinda closed shop. If you're not born rich or a farmer's son, then farming a section of land is a great pipe dream."

"But I'm here, now," Wilf says. "Selling is the problem now. I don't care if the price is down, this year's crop oughta be sold. You know, I get thirty to thirty-five bushels of number two wheat here for every acre of God's dust. I take it to the elevator and the man says he's got bins for only number four wheat. What do I do? Take that wheat home? No, I give it to him for the same price he pays for number four."

"Aren't you getting cheated?"

"Sometimes, maybe; mostly not. But the thing is, that wheat is sold. I can go home and grow some more."

The combine roars steadily, sliding mile-long swathes of yellow down its busy gut. You can see almost forever in any direction except down. There's nothing small about anything here. Nothing defeatist. Sell the wheat and to hell with the price. Grow more, keep it coming, feed the world.

Manitoba

A survivor of the Northwest Rebellion of 1885, now a very old man, was still living in Winnipeg in 1971. Duncan McLean was only eight years old when he was captured by Big Bear and Wandering Spirit. I went to see old Duncan at Gray's Travel Service, where I'd been told he was employed. The man at the travel agency desk said McLean wasn't in just then. I went back again later and was told the same thing. The third time I went back I had a flash of insight. I said to the man at the travel agency, "You're Duncan McLean, aren't you?"

He gave me an odd look and kind of bristled. Then he said, "If you think I'm going to admit that I was a prisoner of Big Bear during the Northwest Rebellion when I'm here selling jet air travel tickets to Rome and Paris, then you're much mistaken." He had a point.

Duncan McLean seemed only about seventy-five at most when I went to see him, but he was ninety-four. And he seemed to sense how I felt about him—living history and that sort of thing—perhaps with a slight resentment. I thought of him in connection with the French and English fur traders of those early days, wandering the prairie of Rupert's Land. But old Duncan fitted no stereotype. He was a snappy dresser, grey pinstripe suit and stylish satin tie making him an ancient man-about-town. Something inside me chortled about this, but I was half-reverent at the same time. It's silly, but I thought: touch the hand that touched the hand of Wandering Spirit and Louis Riel, even if this guy never did touch them.

We drank some coffee and McLean loosened up a little, but not much. What about fear? I said. But even as an eight-year-old, his mother pregnant, his whole family prisoners of hostile Indians who had already murdered several whites, the small boy who became this formidable old man said he was never afraid.

"There was no time for that. You have to remember that the Indians were trying to keep ahead of the white men who were chasing them. And we had to keep up with the Indians, even as prisoners. If we hadn't it would have meant starvation in that wild bush country." He stopped to think back eighty-six years, then said reflectively, "Once I saw an old woman hanging from a tree by a rope. She'd killed herself."

"Why?"

"Couldn't keep up with her people, just too fat and old." McLean didn't say any more about that and didn't need to. But the story turned time around for me: a swift picture of the dead Indian woman formed in my mind, swaying slightly in the wind as she hung on a cottonwood tree. Old Duncan was still silent when I left.

Ontario

Rural Ontario is a nice place to visit. It's also a nice place to live. My wife and I built a house on Roblin Lake near Ameliasburgh twenty years ago, and the "natives" still regard us as outsiders. People around there have voted Conservative since the last shot was fired in the American Revolution, which was when the United Empire Loyalists first started to arrive. And I have no doubt that those first arrivals looked snootily down their noses at the last johnny-come-latelies.

We built the house with a pile of used lumber bought in nearby Belleville, then went inside to wait out the winter. We had no electricity or plumbing. Three oil lamps were required to read a book, and I chopped through three and four-foot-thick ice for water come February and March. An ancient iron cookstove was the only heat source. In really cold weather, I set the alarm clock for every two hours so that I could climb out of bed and stoke the stove. The neighbours, of course, thought I was plumb crazy and my wife even crazier to stay with me.

But while living there—trapped, if you like—I was forced to explore my own immediate surroundings. In 1957 the old Roblin gristmill was still standing—an enormous ruined hulk four stories high, with three-foot-thick stone walls. I poked into every corner of that mill, stepping gingerly over black holes in the floor that dropped forty feet straight down, marvelling at the twenty-four-inch-wide boards from vanished green forests. Old Owen Roblin built that gristmill in 1842. Around 1960 they tore out its liver and lights, installing them in Black Creek Pioneer Village just outside Toronto for the edification of tourists.

Wandering the roads on foot or driving when we had money for gas, I got interested in old architecture – not as an expert, but with the idea that houses express the character of long-dead owners and builders. Gingerbread woodwork on a white frame house, for instance: the exact spot where a nineteenth-century man worked an hour longer than he had to because he got interested and forgot about money. That lost nineteenth-century hour is still visible at one corner of the house.

I keep finding roads I never noticed before, even after all these years of being an outsider – as if some celestial roads department built them last night in the dark of the moon. Leafy and overgrown some of them, fading to a green dead end at run-down farmhouses, abandoned long since but still containing the map of people's lives. Roads like tunnels under trees so thick that the sun shatters into splinters among black branches. Country roads have this endearing quality of never going anywhere important, certainly not to a city; of being an end in themselves, as if at any place where you might care to stop the car you have already arrived.

Quebec

Montreal always seems to me an overwhelmingly large metropolitan centre. But Quebec City is a step back in time; everything already happened and then stopped so that you can see the result. Even the tourists here are not quite so hell-bent for heaven.

In bright metallic fall sunshine, an elevator connecting the Lower Town and Upper Town grumbles and clanks between the two worlds. Above it's touristy; below, it's still touristy –

but with a difference. Around the Chateau Frontenac Hotel, visitors are in their element; in the Lower Town they are on the outside of things, essentially sightseers on the lookout for something picturesque to remember when they get back home.

I am also a tourist, looking for handles for my memory to hold on to. Here on the waterfront – ships loading and unloading, lovers holding hands with their eyes, old stone buildings protruding from past to present, the quintessentially French feeling of the place – dates tick-tock through my mind like little tricolour flags.

Statues of Wolfe and Montcalm on Grande Allée, the Plains of Abraham surrounded by churches and hotels. French-Canadian history, which joins and becomes my own history in 1759 – you have to think of Quebec that way, with a whole net of capillaries and nerves stretching back to the past, woven into the body of Canada as well as into our own bodies, countless invisible threads binding us together in ways that we don't even know about. Which is a point I think the *séparatistes* pass over in silence – the point that the French-Canadian past and the English-Canadian past converge and join to exactly the degree that the spinal cord and pelvic arch of this country's creation belong to both of us.

New Brunswick

In Saint John I intend to just wander the streets, being a ghostly observer of things. But a gale blows in from the sea at forty miles per hour, and even keeping to the sidewalk gets difficult. In the Loyalist Burying Ground I feel transient as thistledown in this wind; the dead are anchored permanently in the nineteenth century. Full summer brings office and factory workers here to eat their lunches in the green shade, for this is a cemetery without walls, right in the downtown area.

I remember Alden Nowlan, the Maritime poet, talking about the kind of vitality people down here have: "I grew up in Hartland, in midwestern New Brunswick, where they have that long covered bridge that's in tourist folders. The kind of place where everyone knows everything about everybody else. The basic kind of life. Farmers and fishermen and working in the woods. Most of them did a little of everything to scratch out a living. And never a very good living. Fights breaking out at dances. What the new schoolteacher was like. The kind of life stuff I try to get into my poems. That wild vitality you see here."

I wander through the Farmer's Market on Charlotte Street, where big orange lobsters stare menacingly at me from white porcelain, beside mobs of periwinkles and clams. I watch the people, trying to see them as Alden Nowlan does. In the harbour a few blocks away, freighters are loading and unloading. The sun sneaks out of shredded clouds, a bit afraid that it may be blown away by the gusting wind.

The Reversing Falls on the St. John River, Martello Tower, the 1810 Loyalist House and Saint John drydock – I've visited all these before and don't feel like retracing my steps. Instead, just by walking and looking at people, I get a feeling of this city by the sea, as if using tracing paper over something I wanted to remember. It's a slightly poorer area than central Canada, but one with its own vitality, its own sturdiness of character instilled by sea and land.

Prince Edward Island

You can see all of Prince Edward Island in one glance from an aeroplane. Not a huge continent or a world, but something the eye and mind can grasp and hold onto. Potato counties and townships at the sea's edge. Dark red soil laid out in squares. Summer crops harvested now and the land nearly naked.

Since I'm Island-born home's as precise
as if a mumbly old carpenter,
shoulder-straps crossed wrong,
laid it out,
refigured to the last three-eighths of a shingle.

That's what poet Milton Acorn wrote about his home island and, looking down from an aeroplane, it's like a big backyard, an outdoor livingroom, a calm place where nobody hurries.

I wander the streets of Charlottetown, past white frame mansions that potatoes built in the nineteenth century; the parliament buildings, where a war was raging about local schools being turned over to the provincial government, making people afraid that their taxes will go up. The province is like a miniature of the country as a whole. But things are slower here and not ashamed to be quaint. Jack McAndrew, the barrel-chested man who was then director of Charlottetown Festival, says: A man is not depersonalized here; he can be involved and make his personality felt still." I think the whole island feels about the rest of Canada the way one PEI voter felt about the political candidate he didn't intend to vote for: "Good luck to you, anyway."

Nova Scotia

From Sydney on Cape Breton Island, I drove thirty miles south to the fishing village of Gabarus. It's a scattered settlement of white frame houses strung out along the edge of a bay open directly to the sea, and it's more or less typical of the small villages on this stretch of Nova Scotia coast. When I got there, thirty-foot waves were leaping right out of the water like white animals and a gale of wind was blowing. Landing stages were empty and the village seemed deserted. But it turned out that everyone was at the general store, waiting for the mail from Sydney.

I spent the whole day talking to fishermen and drinking coffee. Any stereotypes that I had imagined them to fit disappeared as quickly as the coffee. You know the idea: identical fishermen dressed in oilskins selling cod-liver oil, as shown on some bottle label. The fishermen of Gabarus are mixed fishermen, like mixed farmers, harvesting lobster, cod, mackerel, or whatever there is. One thing they do have in common: all are over sixty, some well over seventy.

Young men of the village all move away to cities to make a better living, and these aging men I talked to are probably the last of their kind.

So here's Trueman: dark brown face with deep lines, and something in his manner that says he'll always take a chance. In fact, Trueman is the only man left with nets still out. When the wind cuts down by five miles an hour, he'll be driving his Cape Island boat to sea again to retrieve the nets.

Albert is another sixty-year-old. But all these men look ten or fifteen years younger than their age. Albert fares pretty well with his life. He has a modern house, a new boat that cost some $5,000, and a walkie-talkie over which he talks to his wife ashore whenever they feel companionable. Once, when he ran out of gas, the walkie talkie may have saved his life. Such gadgets are not luxuries among men who fish the ice-cold Atlantic – merely necessities that not all of them are able to afford.

No, fishermen are not stereotypes in oilskins, but there is something common to all of them. I cudgel my brain to figure out what it is. Maybe a calm and quiet around them. Maybe a similarity to the sea itself. They are not animated and excitable men. They do not gesture much with their hands. Maybe you can say about fishermen that the flutter and excitement of verbal fireworks are for children. They are not children, and there is a dark constancy about them. It is for the long haul and has more to do with an essential quiet, as if life is more important than the words attempting to describe it.

Before driving back to Sydney, I had to sit down for a meal of breaded cods' tongues. They wouldn't allow me to leave the village without having eaten. Now, those cods' tongues imbued me with a certain amount of suspicion. Breaded, they look like any other food that's breaded, but an overactive imagination pictured myself talking to other codfish beneath the sea. I might burst out at table with a fishy remark and never know it except for the surprised laughter all around me. I ate them anyway, and they were tender and delicious. I had two helpings.

Newfoundland

On the ferry slip at Sydney, N.S., I watched the big ships
leave for Port-aux-Basques in Newfoundland. Five years
earlier my wife and I had driven a truck camper to Newfoundland. We had gone up the Great Northern Peninsula,
stopping overnight in gravel quarries and clearings beside
the road, buying cod for three-and-a-half cents a pound and
halibut for ten cents from fishermen on the beach, eating
raspberries from scarlet bushes, myself having an occasional
libation of Newfie Screech to aid navigation. It tastes so bad
that you can't feel any bumps on the road, unpaved on that
particular alcoholic route.

The reason for our Newfoundland trip was Vikings. Ten
centuries ago they landed at a point near L'Anse aux Mead-
ows on the northern tip of the island, driving west through
storm and ice from Greenland in oared longships to the Labrador coast. Maybe it was Leif the Lucky who landed in
Newfoundland. Nobody really knows now. A thousand
years of silence have intervened. But driving up the wooded,
sea-lined coastal road, my thoughts were full of horned helmets, Vikings drinking mead and yelling "skoal!" at Beo-
thuk Indians, cutting down the local timber and generally
making a helluva racket.

Helge Ingstad, a Norwegian archaeologist-explorer, had
just finished excavating the site of what might have been
Leif the Lucky's settlement. I had wanted to meet Ingstad.
And now the trip remains in my mind as a mixture of raspberries and codfish, Ingstad (we had coffee with him) and
Screech; also Vikings and the dark shadowy faces of Beo-
thuk Indians vanished from earth in the nineteenth century.

In Newfoundland there are lakes surrounded by trees surrounded by water surrounded by clouds, places that seem to
have been taken out of a peaceful territory in your own
mind. But Sydney is the end of the line for me this time.
There remains only the hippety-hop flight back to Montreal
and the train rumbling west from there with the rhythm of
bare bones on steel. At such times I never feel that there is a

point-of-no-return. There is a kind of joy about both going and coming that stems from making the map of yourself on paper coincide with a 5,000-mile-wide country. Of course it never coincides: all you can do is hint at something much larger than yourself. But I feel lucky that I'm able to try.

About the Author

Born in Wooler, Ontario in 1918, Al Purdy trekked west by rails during the Great Depression and served six years in the RCAF during the Second World War. He has worked at a wide variety of jobs up to the early sixties and has since made his living as a writer, editor and poet. Al has owned a taxi business in Belleville, introduced a union in a Vancouver mattress factory, roamed through northern BC, visited Cuba, wandered around Turkey, Italy, England and Greece, and lived with Eskimos on an island in Cumberland Sound in the Canadian Arctic.

He has been awarded Canada Council Fellowships, the A.J.M. Smith Award, a Centennial Medal in 1967, and has won the Governor-General's Award for Poetry. In addition to his poetry, he has written radio and TV plays, which have been produced by the CBC, and articles for magazines.